Wit
&
Wisdom

# Wit & Wisdom

## CHARLIE "T." JONES & BOB PHILLIPS

**HARVEST HOUSE PUBLISHERS**
Eugene, Oregon 97402

**WIT AND WISDOM**

Copyright © 1977 by Harvest House Publishers
Eugene, Oregon 97402
Formerly called *The Fun Joke Book*

Library of Congress Catalog Card Number 76-53067
ISBN 0-89081-235-7

**Printed in the United States of America.**

## ABSENT-MINDED

Did you hear about the absent-minded professor who:

Returned from lunch and saw a sign on his door, "Back in 30 minutes," and sat down to wait for himself?

Slammed his wife and kissed the door?

Got up and struck a match to see if he had blown out the candle?

## ACCURACY

Even a stopped clock is right twice a day.

## ACE

Damon Runyon used to tell this story on how he got his first newspaper job. It happened in Denver. He sat in the outer office patiently waiting while an office boy carried his request to be seen by the busy editor.

In about ten minutes the boy came back and said, "He wants you to send in a card." Runyon had no card, but being resourceful, he reached into his pocket and pulled out a deck of cards. From the deck he carefully extracted an ace and said, "Give him this."

He got in and he got the job.

## ACHIEVEMENT

I feel that the greatest reward for doing is the opportunity to do more.                Jonas Salk

If you want a place in the sun, you have to expect some blisters.

Achievement is helping a person find out what he needs, then helping him to find the best way to get it.

## ACQUAINTANCE

Jay:   I understand you have a speaking acquaintance with her.

Bill:   Merely a listening acquaintance.

## ADAM

Adam was the first man to know the meaning of rib roast.

The best check-writing machine was made from Adam's rib.

## ADMIRATION

Courageous foe is more to be admired than cowardly friend.

Admiration is the daughter of ignorance.

Distance is a great promoter of admiration.

A fool always finds a greater fool to admire him.

The feeling of delight that another person resembles us.

Admiration begins where acquaintance ceases.

## ADVANTAGE

Every disadvantage has its advantage.

## ADVERSITY

The brook would lose its song if we removed the rocks.

Gold is tried by fire, brave men by adversity.

Seneca

There's no sense in advertising your troubles—there's no market for them.

The darker the day, the more we must pray. The darker the days, the more we should praise.

You are a poor specimen if you can't stand the pressure of adversity.

## ADVERTISING

Doing business without advertising is like winking at a girl in the dark. You know what you are doing, but nobody else does.

Samson had the right idea about advertising. He took two columns and brought down the house.

## ADVICE

Timely advice is as lovely as golden apples in a silver basket.                    Proverbs 25:11

Is it possible to expect mankind to take advice when they will not so much as take warning?
                                                              Swift

He is bad that will not take advice, but he is a thousand times worse who takes every advice.

If you are looking for advice; stay away from fools.                    Proverbs 14:7

Everyone enjoys giving good advice, and how wonderful it is to be able to say the right thing at the right time!                    Proverbs 15:23

Ability to give wise advice satisfies like a good meal.                    Proverbs 18:20

Get all the advice you can and be wise the rest of your life.                    Proverbs 19:20

The best way to succeed in this world is to act on the advice you give to others.

Perhaps one of the reasons why we get so much free advice is that it's easier than helping.

Never trust the advice of a man in difficulties.

A fool thinks he needs no advice, but a wise man listens to others. Proverbs 12:15

People who offer good advice always offer it in the big economy size.

Advice is like snow; the softer it falls, the longer it dwells upon, and the deeper it sinks into the mind. Coleridge

If you wish good advice, consult an old man.

Only a fool despises his father's advice; a wise son considers each suggestion.

Proverbs 15:5

There is an old story of an Eastern merchant who was about to send his eldest son forth into the world. "My son," said the merchant, "there are two precepts I would have you keep ever in mind. The first of these is, 'Always keep your word once you have given it.' "
"Yes, Father," said the son.
"And the second?"
"Never give it."

## AFFECTION

Caresses, expressions of one sort or another, are necessary to the life of the affections as leaves are to the life of a tree. If they are wholly restrained, love will die at the roots.

Above all else, guard your affections. For they influence everything else in your life.

Proverbs 4:23

## AFFLICTION

Affliction, like the iron-smile, shapes as it smites.

Affliction is God's shepherd dog to drive us back to the fold.

The gem cannot be polished without friction, nor man perfected without trials.

As sure as God puts His children into the furnace of affliction He will be with them in it.

Charles Haddon Spurgeon

## AGNOSTIC

A person who says that he knows nothing about God and, when you agree with him, he becomes angry.

Agnostic is Latin for ignoramus.

## AGGRAVATING

Think twice before you speak and you may say something even more aggravating.

## AGREE

When two men in a business always agree, one of them is unnecessary. William Wrigley, Jr.

## AGREEMENT

You may easily play a joke on a man who likes to argue — agree with him.

There is no conversation more boring than the one where everybody agrees.

He that complies against his will is of his own opinion still. Samuel Butler

## AHEAD

A good thing to have.

## AIM

In great attempts it is glorious even to fail.

## AIR-CONDITIONED

Why is it a businessman will go from his air-conditioned house to his air-conditioned office in his air-conditioned car, then go to a health club and pay $50 an hour to sweat?

## ALLOWANCE

Son to father, "About my allowance, Pop. It's fallen below the national average for teenagers."

## ALONE

A person who is alone isn't necessarily in good company.

## AMERICA

A citizen of America will cross the ocean to fight for democracy, but won't cross the street to vote in a national election.

America is the country where you buy a lifetime supply of aspirin for one dollar and use it up in two weeks.                    John Barrymore

## AMIABILITY

An inexhaustible good nature is one of the most precious gifts of heaven, spreading itself like oil over the troubled sea of thought, and keeping the mind smooth and equable in the roughest weather.                    Washington Irving

## AMMONIA

Lisa:  Don't you know the difference between ammonia and pneumonia?

Chris: Sure, one comes in bottles and the other in chests.

## ANGER

He is a fool who cannot be angry; but he is a wise man who will not.

Whenever you are angry, be assured that it is not only a present evil, but that you have increased a habit.                    Epictetus

Keep cool; anger is not an argument.
                    Daniel Webster

Anger is as a stone cast into a wasp's nest.

The greatest remedy for anger is delay.

Seneca

When a man is wrong and won't admit it, he always gets angry.

I was angry with my friend, I told my wrath, my wrath did end.
I was angry with my foe.
I told it not, my wrath did grow.

William Blake

Anger blows out the lamp of the mind.

Robert Green Ingersol

A little pot
Is soon hot.

## APATHY

The No. 1 problem in our country is apathy . . . But who cares!

## APOSTLE PAUL

Question: When was the Apostle Paul a baker?
Answer:   When he went to Philippi.

## APPETITE

A well-governed appetite is a great part of liberty.

Seneca

Carry an appetite to God's house, and you will be fed.

## APPLE

Something that was stuck in Adam's throat.

Handsome apples are sometimes sour.

While visiting a friend who was in the hospital, I noticed several pretty nurses, each of whom was wearing a pin designed to look like an apple. I asked one nurse what the pin signified.

"Nothing," she said with a smile. "It's just to keep the doctors away."

## APPOINTMENT

Not keeping an appointment is an act of clear dishonesty. You may as well borrow a person's money as his time.                    Horace Mann

## ARCHAEOLOGIST

A man whose career lies in ruins.

## ARGUMENT

If you really want the last word in an argument, try saying, "I guess you're right."

I always get the better when I argue alone.

Something you do with a fool, but be sure he isn't similarly engaged.

He who establishes his argument by noise and command shows that his reason is weak.

Behind every argument is someone's ignorance.

A long dispute means both parties are wrong.

The only way to get the best of an argument is to avoid it.                    Dale Carnegie

The good man wins his case by careful argument; the evil-minded only wants to fight.
                    Proverbs 13:2

There is no boxing match with only one person.

## ART

If my husband would ever meet a woman on the street who looked like the women in his paintings, he would fall over in a dead faint.

Mrs. Pablo Picasso

Art, like morality, consists in drawing the line somewhere.            Gilbert K. Chesterton

## ASSASSINATION

Assassination: the extreme form of censorship.

George Bernard Shaw

## ATHEISM

Nobody talks so constantly about God as those who insist that there is no God.

I am an atheist, thank God!

An atheist is one point beyond the devil.

Some are atheists only in fair weather.

By night an atheist half believes in a god.

## ATOM

The professor of a technical class was conducting an experiment with atoms. At the end, he commented: "Now observe that at the beginning of this experiment there were twenty-seven atoms. Now there are only twenty-six."

Then he asked, "What happened to that other atom, students?"

After several moments of tense silence, a low voice from the back of the room said, "Nobody leave this room."

## ATTITUDE

As he thinketh in his heart, so is he.

Bible

A relaxed attitude lengthens a man's life; jealousy rots it away. Proverbs 14:30

When we are flat on our backs there is no way to look but up.

Those who wish to sing always find a song.

## AUCTION

Auction — A place where you are liable to get something for nodding.

## BACHELOR

Nancy: What excuse have you for not being married?
Rich: I was born that way.

Joan: "Hasn't Jack ever married?"
Jean: "No, I don't think he intends to, because he's studying for a bachelor's degree."

Bachelor: One who's footloose and fiancee free.

## BAGDAD

What mother did when she met father.

## BAKERY

"You're the object of our confections."

## BALANCED BUDGET

Question: What is a balanced budget?
Answer: When money in the bank and the days of the month come out together.

## BALLET

A little boy who went to the ballet for the first time with his father watched the girls dance around on their toes for a while, and then asked, "Why don't they just get taller girls?"

## BANANA

Dave: If something is yellow and looks like a banana and smells like a banana how do you know if it's really a banana?

Dick: Listen and see if it makes a noise like a banana.

## BARBER

A brilliant conversationalist, who occasionally shaves and cuts hair.

It is getting so a good barber can earn as much per word as an author.

## BARK

Barking dogs never bite . . . while barking.

## BATH

Every man has the right to a Saturday night bath and many need to exercise their rights.

## BEANS

They serve a balanced diet in the Army. Every bean weighs the same.

## BEARD

"Once I had a beard like yours, and when I saw how terrible I looked, I got it cut off."

"I used to have a face like yours, too, and when I saw how terrible it made me look I grew a beard."

## BED

As you make your bed, so you must lie on it.

## BEFRIEND

When befriended, remember it;
When you befriend—forget it

## BEHAVIOR

Behavior is a mirror in which everyone displays his image.

Johann Wolfgang von Goethe

Be nice to people on your way up because you'll meet them on your way down.

The reason the way of the transgressor is hard is because it's so crowded.

The man who wears his pants out before his shoes, makes contact in the wrong places.

Some folks don't have many faults, but they sure make the most of those they've got.

## BEHIND

He who rides behind another does not travel when he pleases.

## BIBLE

Most people are bothered by those passages of Scripture they do not understand, but the passages that bother me are those I do understand.

Mark Twain

Be careful how you live; you may be the only Bible some person ever reads.

Thy word is a lamp unto my feet, and a light unto my path.          Psalms 119:105,KJV

The family Bible can be passed down from generation to generation because it gets so little wear.

Despise God's Word and find yourself in trouble. Obey it and succeed. Proverbs 13:13

But the Word of the Lord endureth forever.
I Peter 1:25, KJV

The reason people are down on the Bible is that they're not up on the Bible.

William Ward Ayer

Sin will keep you from this book. This Book will keep you from sin. Dwight L. Moody

Men do not reject the Bible because it contradicts itself but because it contradicts them.

## BILLS

Woman to bill paying husband: "I slashed expenses last month — everything was charged on one credit card so that it will take only one postage stamp to pay our bills."

We never get anything but sad news out of those envelopes with a window in front.

## BIRTHDAY

Husband to wife: "How do you expect me to remember your birthday when you never look any older?"

## BLAME

He wrecked his car, he lost his job, and yet throughout his life, he took his troubles like a man — he blamed them on his wife!

To err is human; to blame it on the other guy is even more human.

You are not a failure until you blame someone else.

## BLASTS

The number of blasts that come from auto horns in a traffic jam is equal to the sum of the squares at the wheels.

## BLIZZARD

A blizzard is the inside of a fowl.

## BLUNDER

Mark Twain was once asked the difference between a mistake and blunder. He explained it this way. "If you walk into a restaurant and walk out with someone's silk umbrella and leave your own cotton one, that is a mistake. But if you pick up someone's cotton umbrella and leave your own silk one, that's a blunder."

## BOLDNESS

When you cannot make up your mind which of two evenly balanced courses of action you should take — choose the bolder.

## BONE

Some people have a lot of it in their head.

The bone of contention is the jawbone.

I work my head to the bone.

## BOTTLENECK

The bottleneck is always at the top.

## BOY

Boys will be boys, and so will a lot of middle-aged men.

An appetite with a skin pulled over it.

One of the best things in the world to be is a boy; it requires no experience, but needs some practice to be a good one.

## BRAINS

Don: She's a bright girl . . . she has brains enough for two.

Art: Then she's just the girl for you.

"How long can a man live without brains?"
"I don't know. How old are you?"

## BRAVE

It is easy to be brave from a safe distance.

Aesop

## BREVITY

Brevity is a fine thing in a speech.

## BRIDLE

Better a bridle on the tongue than a lash upon the conscience.

## BRIEFLY

After-dinner speaking is the art of saying nothing briefly.

## BUGGY

What some people drive you.

## BULLETIN BOARD

In front of church: "You are not too bad to come in. You are not too good to stay out."

## BULLY

I used to beat up all the kids on the block, except the McKees. I had a little trouble with them. They were boys.

## BUMPER-STICKER

Bumper-sticker slogan in Houston: "Be a Monkey's Uncle! Join the Zoological Society of Houston."

## BUS DRIVER

Definition of a school bus driver: A man who thought he liked children.

## BUS FARE

Jack-in-the-box.

## BUSY

Whoever admits that he is too busy to improve his methods has acknowledged himself to be at the end of his rope. And that is always the saddest predicament which anyone can get into.

J. Ogden Armour

Have you noticed that even the busiest people are never too busy to take time to tell you how busy they are?

## BUTTER

Be not a baker if your head be of butter.

## BUY

If you buy a bad thing you will soon buy again.

## BUYING

She's always for getting. For getting this and for getting that.

## CAIN

Heckler:   Who was Cain's wife?

Preacher: I respect any seeker of knowledge, but I want to warn you, young man, don't risk being lost to salvation by too much inquiring after other men's wives.

## CALM

God promises a safe landing but not a calm passage.

## CANDLE

A candle loses · nothing by lighting another candle.

Don't burn out a candle in search of a pin.

## CAR

Fifteen-year-old Fred: "Dad, the Bible says that if you don't let me have the car, you hate me."

Dad: "Where does it say that?"

Son: "Proverbs 13:24. He that spareth the 'rod' hateth his son."

## CAR SICKNESS
The feeling you get every month when the payment is due.

## CASH
The vanishing American is the one who pays cash for everything he buys.

## CATERPILLAR
Two caterpillars were crawling across the grass when they saw a butterfly flutter past about them. One nudged the other and said, "You couldn't get me up in one of those things for a million dollars!"

## CAUCUS
The part of an animal left for the buzzards.

## CAUTION
It is well to swim with one foot on the ground.

Be slow of tongue and quick of eye.
Miguel de Cervantes

## CENSURE
I find that the pain of a little censure, even when it is unfounded, is more acute than the pleasure of much praise.　Thomas Jefferson

## CHAINS
Men rattle their chains to show that they are free.

## CHAIRMAN
According to Nan Hampton, a chairman of a meeting is like the minor official at a bullfight whose main function is to open and close the gates to let the bull in and out.

## CHANGE
He who would be well served must know when to change his servants.

## CHANNELS

God has given us two hands — one to receive with and the other to give with. We are not cisterns made for hoarding; we are channels made for sharing.                                    Billy Graham

## CHAPPED

Harry: "Please give me a kiss."
Carrie: "My lips are chapped."
Harry: "Well, one more chap won't hurt them."

## CHARACTER

Tears on your pillow will never wash out stains on your character.

Don't envy the lucky fellow whose path is smoothed for him. Pity him. Some day he will seek your favor. Success is the product of character. The development of your character is in your own hands, and poverty plus honest ambition is the best environment for character-building.

When wealth is lost, nothing is lost;
When health is lost, something is lost;
When character is lost, all is lost!

Character is a by-product; it is produced in the great manufacture of daily duty.

The measure of a man's real character is what he would do if he knew he would never be found out.

## CHARITY

Though I speak with the tongues of men and angels and have not charity, I am become as sounding brass, or a tinkling cymbal.

I Corinthians 13:1, KJV

## CHEAT

He that's cheated twice by the same man is an accomplice with the cheater.

He that will cheat at play
Will cheat you any way.

Bob: Did you pass your finals?
Bill:  And how.
Bob: Were they easy?
Bill:  Dunno . . . ask Jim.

## CHECK-UP

The customer brought his new car into the dealer for its 1,000 mile check-up.

"Is there anything the matter with it?" inquired the service manager.

"Well," replied the customer, "There's only one part of it that doesn't make a noise, and that's the horn."

## CHEWING TOBACCO

New fishing lure made up of chewing tobacco. How does it work? Well, when the fish comes up to spit, you hit him with with an oar.

## CHILDREN

Satan keeps school for neglected children.

Father:  "Why are you always at the bottom of your class?"
Dennis:  "It doesn't make any difference. They teach the same thing at both ends.

"Billy, get your little brother's hat out of that mud puddle." "I can't ma, he's got it strapped too tight under his chin."

It was Washington's birthday. Johnny called over to his neighbor, Danny, "Say, aren't you going to put up your flag today?"

"Naw," answered Danny. "I don't even put the flag up for my own birthday."

If children did not ask questions, they would never learn how little adults know.

The trouble with your children is that when they're not being a lump in your throat, they're being a pain in your neck.

The greatest aid to adult education is children.

## CHIP

A chip on the shoulder indicates there is wood higher up.

## CHIPS

A man arrested for gambling came before the judge. "We weren't playing for money," he explained to the judge. "We were just playing for chips."

"Chips are just the same as money," the judge sternly replied.

"I fine you fifteen dollars."

The defendant looked sad, then slowly reached into his pocket and handed the judge three blue chips.

## CHOICE

Between two evils, choose neither, between two goods, choose both.

In literature, as in love, we are astonished at the choice made by other people.

When you have to make a choice and don't make it, that in itself is a choice.    William James

"One can decide a lot of things, but personal choices are hard. I tend to wait until one alternative is no longer available, and then inform myself that I have chosen."

## CHOOSE

One should choose for a wife only such a woman as he would choose for a friend, were she a man.    Joubert

## CHRIST

Christ sends none away empty but those who are full of themselves.

Christ never wrote a tract, but He went about doing good.

## CHRISTIANITY

The trouble with some of us is that we have been inoculated with small doses of Christianity which keeps us from catching the real thing.

If a man cannot be a Christian in the place where he is, he cannot be a Christian anywhere.
    Henry Ward Beecher

There is one single fact which we may oppose to all the wit and argument of infidelity, namely, that no man ever repented of being a Christian on his death bed.

Christianity has not been tried and found wanting; it has been found difficult and not tried.
    Chesterton

Christian: One who believes that the New Testament is a divinely inspired book admirably suited to the spiritual needs of his neighbors.

Christianity is bread for daily use, not cake for special occasions.

## CHURCH BULLETIN BOARDS

Come in and have your faith lifted.

Come in and let us prepare you for your finals.

A miser is a rich pauper.

Ask about our pray-as-you-go plan.

We hold sit-in demonstrations every Sunday.

No matter how much you nurse a grudge it won't get better.

Start living to beat hell.

If some people lived up to their ideals they would be stooping.

Everything you always wanted to know about heaven and hell but were afraid to ask.

Pray up in advance.

Patience is the ability to stand something as long as it happens to the other fellow.

Think twice before you speak and you may say something even more aggravating.

## CITIZENS

Whatever makes men good Christians, makes them good citizens.                    Daniel Webster

## CITIZENSHIP

Voting is the least arduous of a citizen's duties. He has the prior and harder duty of making up his mind.

## CLAMDIGGER

A person who is mussel bound.

## CLASS

All mankind is divided into three classes: those that are immovable, those that are movable, and those that move.

## CLEANLINESS

Cleanliness is next to impossible.

Cleanliness is next to Godliness, but in childhood it's next to impossible.

**CLIMB**

He who climbs too high may have a fall;
But better a fall than not to climb at all.

**CLOTHES**

Teenager, Mary, was in tears the other night because she had nothing to wear for her date. All her sweat shirts were in the wash.

**COACH**

A coach was being congratulated on having a lifetime contract. "I guess it's all right," he said. "But I remember another guy with a lifetime contract. Had a bad year, and the president called him in, pronounced him dead, and fired him."

**COFFIN**

My brother has invented a new coffin. It just goes over the head. It's for people who are dead from the neck up. Do you want to buy one?

**COLD**

Question: Which travels faster . . . heat or cold?
Answer:  Heat . . . because you can catch cold easily.

**COLLEGE**

Dad doesn't waste words when he writes a letter. One he sent to me at Simmons College was enclosed with air fare home for Christmas vacation. The letter read, "Dear Sue, Here's some bread so you can get back to the breadbox."

Gal: And just why did you have to cut in while I was dancing with a four-letter man? You're just a freshman.

Guy: I'm sorry, ma'am, but I'm working my way through college and your partner was waving a five-dollar bill at me.

Freshman:   I don't know.
Sophomore: I'm not prepared.
Junior:       I don't remember.
Senior:       I don't believe I can add anything
                 to what has already been said.

Father:     My son just received his B.A.
Neighbor: I suppose now he'll be looking for a
                 Ph.D.
Father:     No, now he's looking for a J-O-B.

My son went to college and received an M.A.
and a B.A. but his P.A. still supports him.

Letter from son at school:
   Dear Dad,
   Gue$$ what I need mo$t. That'$ right. $end it
$oon.
                         Be$t Wi$he$
                              Jay
Reply:
   Dear Jay,
   NOthing ever happens here. We kNOw you
like school. Write aNOther letter soon. Mom was
asking about you at NOon.
   NOw I have to say good-by,
                              Dad

## COLLEGE-CHEER
   The check from home.

## COMEDIAN
   A person who has a good memory for old jokes.

## COMFORT
   No man's head aches while he comforts
another.

## COMPARTMENT
   One woman to another: "My purse has a com-

partment I call the Bermuda Triangle. Items from other compartments drop into it and disappear."

## COMPETITION

Two barber shops were in red hot competition. One put up a sign advertising haircuts for 75 cents. His competitor put up one that read, "We repair 75 cent haircuts."

The reason why men who mind their own business succeed is because they have so little competition.

## COMPLAINT

The wheel that squeaks the loudest is the first to be replaced.

The wheel that squeaks the loudest is the one that gets the grease.                    Josh Billings

Waiter:  We haven't had a complaint in twenty-five years.
Customer: No wonder. The customers all starve to death before they are served.

## COMPLIMENT

I have been complimented many times and they always embarrass me; I always feel that they have not said enough.                    Mark Twain

Whenever a man's friends begin to compliment him about looking young, he may be sure that they think he is growing old.

Washington Irving

## COMPUTER

If computers get too powerful, we can organize them into committees. That'll do them in.

To err is human; to really foul things up requires a computer.

## COMMAND

He who can commands, and he who will obeys.

## COMMITTEE

A committee is a group that keeps minutes and loses hours.                    Milton Berle

To get something done a committee should consist of three men, two of whom are absent.

If you want to kill any idea in the world today, get a committee working on it.

Never fear that machines may get too powerful. When they do, we can organize them into committees.

A committee is a group of people who talk for hours to produce a result called minutes.

Committee is a noun of multitude, signifying many, but not signifying much.

## COMMON BOND

The common bond of rebels is their guilt. The common bond of godly people is good will.

## COMMUNISM

Communism has nothing to do with love. Communism is an excellent hammer which we use to destroy our enemy.                    Mao Tse-tung

A communist is like a crocodile: when it opens its mouth you cannot tell whether it is trying to smile or preparing to eat you up.
                                    Winston Churchill

The theory of Communism may be summed up in one sentence:
Abolish all private property.                    Karl Marx

## CONCLUSION

The troops were being taught to jump from a plane.

"What if my parachute doesn't open?" asked one rookie.

"That," said the instructor, "is known as jumping to a conclusion."

Jumping at conclusions is not half as good exercise as digging for facts.

A doctor, appearing as an expert witness on behalf of a man injured in a car accident, was being badgered by an overbearing attorney.

"You say, Doctor, that you're familiar with symptoms of brain concussion?"

"That's correct," replied the Doctor.

"Well tell me, Doctor," continued the attorney; "If you and I were riding in a car, and another car struck us and our heads bumped together, is it your opinion that we would suffer a concussion?"

"It's my opinion," replied the Doctor, "that I would and you wouldn't."

## CONFERENCE

An experienced executive said it, "A conference is the confusion of one man multiplied by the number present."

## CONFESSION

The confession of evil works is the first beginning of good works.                St. Augustine

Confession is the first step to repentance.

## CONNECTIONS

Many a live wire would be dead without connections.

## CONQUER

Conquer a dog before you contend with a lion.

## CONSCIENCE

When a person feels that his thinking is getting broader, it is more likely that his conscience is stretching.

My conscience hath a thousand several tongues.                                    Shakespeare

Conscience doesn't keep you from doing anything; it just keeps you from enjoying it.

Conscience is what hurts when everything else feels so good.

A good conscience is a continual Christmas.
Benjamin Franklin

Keep conscience clear, then never fear.

A man's conscience is the Lord's searchlight exposing his hidden motives.      Proverbs 20:27

## CONSISTENT

The only advice I get about raising children is to be consistent. But how can I be consistent? They never do the same thing twice.

## COOK

Bride:   "The two best things I cook are meat-
loaf and apple dumplings."
Groom: "Well, which is this?"

## COOPERATION

An old ferryman painted the word "Faith" on one oar and "Works" on the other. When asked the reason he explained: "To make a passage across the river you need both oars. See where 'Faith' without 'Works' takes us." The ferryman slipped one oar and turned with "Faith" only, and went around and around in a circle. "Now let us try 'Works' without 'Faith.' We make just a little headway; and it is just the same in the journey of life."

## CORRUPTION

When you remove dross from silver, you have sterling ready for the silversmith. When you remove corrupt men from the king's court, his reign will be just and fair.          Proverbs 25:4-5

## COUNTERSIGN

Unless you have the extra cash on hand, don't countersign a note. Why risk everything you own? They'll even take your bed.
                              Proverbs 22:26-27

## COURT

. . . A place where they dispense with justice.

The penalty for laughing in a courtroom is six months in jail; if it were not for this penalty, the jury would never hear the evidence.

## COUNSEL

Too much taking counsel ends in doing nothing.

In great straits and when hope is small, the boldest counsels are the safest.

## COUNTENANCE

A happy face means a glad heart; a sad face means a breaking heart.          Proverbs 15:13

## COURTESY

We must be as courteous to a man as we are to a picture, which we are willing to give the advantage of a good light.          Ralph Waldo Emerson

## COURTSHIP

A courtship begins when a man whispers sweet nothings, and ends when he says nothing sweet.

In courtship a man pursues a woman until she catches him.

Every young woman knows when the right guy comes along because he tells her.

A young man had been courting a girl for quite some time, and trying to no avail to get her consent to marriage. He finally confided to her that "my elderly father is quite sickly and will probably die soon. When that happens I will be a millionaire."
Two days later she became his stepmother.

## COVETOUSNESS

Covetousness is the punishment of the rich.

## COWARD

A hundred times in life a coward dies.

## C.P.N.

Myrlene: He's a C.P.N.
Sharon: You mean C.P.A. Certified Public
         Accountant.
Myrlene: No . . . C.P.N. Contstant Pain in the
        Neck.

## CREASE

When packing vacation clothes, take the line of crease resistance.

## CREDIT

The world's poorest credit risk is the man who agrees to pay a stranger's debts.   Proverbs 27:13

Credit is like chastity, they can both stand temptation better than suspicion.          Josh Billings

No man's credit is as good as his money.

Be sure you know a person well before you vouch for his credit! Better refuse than suffer later.
Proverbs 11:15

The surest way to establish your credit is to work yourself into the position of not needing any.

The man had barely paid off his mortgage on the house when he mortgaged it again to buy a car and, not long after, he borrowed to build a garage. His banker hesitated, and said, "If I do make this new loan, how will you buy gas for the car?"

"It seems to me," replied the borrower curtly, "that a fellow who owns a big house, a car and garage should be able to get credit for gasoline."

Glen: Are you still living within your income?
Rich: No. It's all I can do to live within my credit.

## CRIME

Set a thief to catch a thief.

Few men have virtue to withstand the highest
bidder. George Washington

We don't seem to be able to check crime, so
why not legalize it and then tax it out of business.
Will Rogers

## CRITICIZE

Criticize by creating. Michelangelo

## CRITICISM

When some people abuse you, they can't
understand why you resent "constructive
criticism."

When someone says, "I do not wish to appear
critical," it means he is going to let you have it.

Heat hardens clay, but melts wax. It tempers
steel but softens lead. The hot sun ripens fruit and
grain, but withers and blasts the cut flowers and
tender plants. Wintry blasts work havoc with summer annuals, but toughen the fiber of the mighty
oaks. The difference in results is not with the exter-
nal agent but with the inherent qualities of the
receiving object.

Every person who attempts to do anything
worthwhile has to learn to take criticism, constructive or otherwise. Often those who accomplish
most in the long run come in for the most criticism.

## CROSSWORD PUZZLE

Did you hear about the crossword puzzle addict
who died and was buried six feet down and three
across?

## CRUEL

One of the ill effects of cruelty is that it makes the bystanders cruel.

## CRY

If at first you don't succeed, cry, cry again.

## CUBIC

Question: What is a cubic?
Answer: The language spoken in Cuba.

## CULTURE

The man had been dragged to a classical violin concert by his culture-minded wife. Trying to teach him some of the finer points she whispered during the concert, "What do you think of his execution?"

"I'm all for it," replied the husband

## CUPID

Cupid's dart hurt more coming out than going in.

## CURRENT

It takes a strong man to swim against the current; and dead fish will float with it.

## CURSES

Curses, like young chickens, still come home to roost.

## CYNIC

A cynic is a man who, when he smells flowers, looks around for a coffin.

One who is married.

A cynic is a man who knows the price of everything, and the value of nothing.
Oscar Wilde

## DAMP

Pam: Why was your letter so damp?
Rosie: Postage due, I guess.

## DANCE

Rod:   I'm through with that girl.
Doug: Oh, why?
Rod:   She asked me if I danced.
Doug: Well, what's wrong with that?
Rod:   I was dancing with her when she asked me.

## DANDRUFF

Small, whitish scales trying to get ahead.

## DANGER

There's nothing so comfortable as a small bankroll; a big one is always in danger.

Wilson Mizner

Anger is only one letter short of danger.

Facing danger is not courage unless one knows the danger faced.

## DAY

I'd enjoy the day more if it started later.

One of these days is none of these days.

What a day may bring, a day may take away.

## DEATH

There'll be many a dry eye at his death.

Is death the last sleep? No, it is the last and final awakening.                          Sir Walter Scott

## DEAF AND DUMB

Did you hear about the deaf and dumb guy who wore boxing gloves to bed so he wouldn't talk in his sleep.

## DEAR JOHN

One of Joe's bunk-mates broke up with his girlfriend. The girlfriend wrote demanding that he return her photograph immediately. The soldier borrowed a collection of several pictures of various girls and sent them to his ex-sweetheart with her photo tucked in among them. He enclosed a note:

"Dear Mildred, pick out yours. I have forgotten what you look like."

## DECISIONS

One moment may throw down the credit years have built.

Did you hear about the parents who sent their young son to camp to learn to make decisions of his own?

He did. The second day there he decided to come home.

## DECEIVE

Oh, what a tangled web we weave,
When first we practice to deceive.        Scott

The greatest deceiver — one who deceives himself.

Oh, what a tangled web we weave,
When once we venture to deceive!

R.D. She said I'm interesting, brave and intelligent.
Bob: You should never go steady with a girl who deceives you from the very start.

## DEFEAT

Defeat isn't bitter if you don't swallow it.

Believe you are defeated, believe it long enough, and it is likely to become a fact.
                              Norman Vincent Peale

Politics have become so expensive that it takes a lot of money even to be defeated.

Will Rogers

## DEFENDANT

"You have known the defendant how long?"
"Twelve years."
"Tell the court whether you think he is the type of man who would steal this money or not."
"How much was it?"

## DELINQUENT

When adults act like children, they're silly; when children act like adults, they are delinquent.

## DENSE

Teacher: "What are the people of New York noted for?"
Charlie: "For their stupidity."
Teacher: "Where ever did you get that idea?"
Charlie: "It says here in this book that the population of New York is very dense."

## DEPRESSION

Depressions may bring people closer to the church — but so do funerals.

## DERMATOLOGIST

Dermatologists make rash judgments.

## DESERVE

It is better to deserve without receiving, than to receive without deserving.

## DESIRE

There are two tragedies in life. One is not to get your heart's desire. The other is to get it.

George Bernard Shaw

The reason so few people get what they want is because they don't want hard enough.

If you desire many things, many things will seem but a few.

Lord, grant that I may always desire more than I can accomplish.                    Michelangelo

## DESK

A wastebasket with drawers.

## DETERMINATION

Beware of what you set your mind on for that you will surely become.                    Emerson

No termination without determination.

## DEVIL

Talk of the devil, and his horns appear, says the proverb.                    Samuel Taylor Coleridge

Resist the devil, and he will flee from you.
                    James 4:7, KJV

For where God built a church, there the Devil would also build a chapel.                    Martin Luther

Don't open the door when the Devil looks in at the window.

Why do I believe in the Devil? For three reasons:
1. Because the Bible plainly says he exists.
2. Because I see his work everywhere.
3. Because great scholars have recognized his existence.                    Billy Graham

## DICTATOR

"Do you know who the greatest dictator in the world is?"
"Know him . . . I married him!"

## DIET

The best way to lose weight is to eat all you want of everything you don't like.

A diet is what helps a person gain weight more slowly.

## DIFFICULTY

The occasion is piled high with difficulty, and we must rise high with the occasion.          Lincoln

Looking difficulty squarely in the face will often kill it.

There are two ways of meeting difficulties: you alter the difficulties or you alter yourself meeting them.

## DILIGENCE

The expectations of life depend upon diligence; the mechanic that would perfect his work must first sharpen his tools.

## DINNER

A good dinner sharpens wit, while it softens the heart.

## DIPLOMAT

A diplomat is a man who says you have an open mind instead of telling you that you have a hole in your head.

One who never heard that old joke before.

## DIRT

He who falls in the dirt, the longer he lies the dirtier he is.

## DISAGREE

Man to friend: "By the time I found out my father was right, my son was old enough to disagree with me."

Wife:      I'm afraid the mountain air would disagree with me.
Husband: My dear, it wouldn't dare.

## DISAPPOINTMENT

Too many people miss the silver lining because they're expecting gold.

## DISCIPLINE

Don't fail to correct your children; discipline won't hurt them! They won't die if you use a stick on them! Punishment will keep them out of hell.
Proverbs 23:13-14

Scolding and spanking a child helps him to learn. Left to himself, he brings shame to his mother.
Proverbs 29:15

Discipline your son and he will give you happiness and peace of mind.          Proverbs 29:17

Discipline, like the bridle in the hand of a good rider, should exercise its influence without appearing to do so; should be ever active, both as a support and as a restraint, yet seem to lie easily in hand. It must always be ready to check or to pull up, as occasion may require; and only when the horse is a runaway should the action of the curb be perceptible.

Becky: I see your father raised you properly.
Dave: Raised me? He used to raise me a foot off the floor when he raised me.

A permissive mother said to her wild little son, "Sit down and stop making so much noise."
"No, I won't . . . so there!" said the boy in an impudent tone.
"Stand up, then . . . I will be obeyed!"

Rearing children these days is like drafting a blueprint: you have to know where to draw the line.

## DISCRETION

An ounce of discretion is worth a pound of learning.

Make your affairs known in the marketplace, and one will call them black and another white.

As a jewel of gold in a swine's snout, so is a fair woman which is without discretion.

If you shout a pleasant greeting to a friend too early in the morning, he will count it as a curse!
                                                Proverbs 27:14

## DISCUSSION

A friendly discussion is as stimulating as the sparks that fly when iron strikes iron.
                                                Proverbs 27:17

## DISHONESTY

Don't place too much confidence in the man who boasts of being as honest as the day is long. Wait until you meet him at night.

## DISRESPECT

A man who has made fun of his wife can love her no more.

## DIVORCE

What a holler would ensue if people had to pay the minister as much to marry them as they have to pay a lawyer to get a divorce.

Dopey: "Why did the cow get a divorce?"
Dopier: "She got a bum steer."

One woman I know charged her husband with mental cruelty so severe it caused her to lose 30 pounds. "Divorce granted!" said the judge. "Oh, not yet," the woman pleaded. "First I want to lose another ten pounds."

## DOCTOR

My husband was very sick so we called Doctor Jones. My husband took his medicine and got worse. Then we called Doctor Vernon and my husband took his medicine and he got still worse. We thought he was going to die, so we called Doctor McKee and he was too busy, and finally my husband got well.

Dr. Hanson: So the operation on the man was just in the nick of time?

Dr. Poure:    Yes, in another twenty-four hours he would have recovered.

"Doctor," said the pale-faced man to his physician, "I'm in an awful state! Whenever the phone rings, I almost jump out of my skin. The doorbell gives me the willies. If I see a stranger at the door, I start shaking. I'm even afraid to look at a newspaper. What's come over me, anyway?"

The doctor patted him on the back sympathetically. "There, there, old man. I know what you're going through. My teenaged daughter just learned to drive, too."

Patient: What would you charge to alter my nose?

Doctor: Five hundred dollars.

Patient: Anything cheaper?

Doctor: You can try walking into a telephone pole.

## DOGHOUSE

Mutt hut.

## DOLLAR

Jack of all trades.

## DONKEY

Nothing passes between donkeys but kicks.

If your brother is a donkey, what are you?

## DOUBLE CHIN

He's got a couple of double chins. Every time he talks he broadcasts over short waves.

## DOW JONES AVERAGE

. . . The Dow Jones average is roamin' numerals.

## DRESS

The body is the shell of the soul, and dress the husk of that shell; but the husk often tells what the kernel is.

If honor be your clothing, the suit will last a lifetime; but if clothing be your honor, it will soon be worn threadbare.

Dress changes the manners.

"Have you seen Sally's new dress?"
"No, what does it look like?"
"Well, in many places it's a lot like Sally."

## DRINKING

Whose heart is filled with anguish and sorrow? Who is always fighting and quarreling? Who is the man with bloodshot eyes and many wounds? It is the one who spends long hours in the taverns, trying out new mixtures. Don't let the sparkle and the smooth taste of strong wine deceive you.

Proverbs 23:29-31

## DRIVE

You can do more than strike while the iron is hot; you can make the iron hot by striking.

## DRIVING

Driving Instructor: "What would you do if you were going up an icy hill and the motor stalled and the brakes failed?"

Student: "I'd quickly adjust the rear view mirror."

## DRUMMER

Boss to employee: "You may march to a different drummer, but I want the beat speeded up."

## DRYER

A sign on a dryer in a coin laundry reads: "This dryer is worthless." A sign on the next dryer reads: "This dryer is next to worthless."

## DULL

The trouble with telling a good story is that it reminds the other fellow of a dull one.

## DUMB

I didn't say he was dumb . . . I said he was twenty-years-old before he could wave goodbye.

## DUTY

Best way to get rid of your duties is to discharge them.

I slept, and dreamed that life was Beauty;
I woke, and found that life was Duty.

For strength to bear is found in duty alone, and he is blest indeed who learns to make the joy of others cure his own heartache.

A duty dodged is like a debt unpaid; it is only deferred, and we must come back and settle the account at last.

Do something everyday that you don't want to do; this is the golden rule for acquiring the habit of doing your duty without pain.          Mark Twain

## EARTH

The pagans do not know God, and love only the earth. The Jews know the true God, and love only the earth. The Christians know the true God, and do not love the earth.          Blaise Pascal

## EATING

Eat, drink, and be merry, for tomorrow ye diet.

Doctors say that if you eat slowly you eat less. You certainly will if you are a member of a large family.

He who does not mind his belly will hardly mind anything else.                    Samuel Johnson

When it comes to eating, you can sometimes help yourself more by helping yourself less.
                                    Richard Armour

We used to say, "What's cooking?" when we came home from work. Now it's "What's thawing?"

The proof of the pudding is in the eating.
                                Miguel de Cervantes

If you really want to lose weight, there are only three things you must give up: breakfast, lunch, and dinner.

## ECHOES

There are many echoes in the world, but few voices.

## ECONOMIST

An economist is a person who talks about something he doesn't understand and makes you believe you're ignorant.

## EDUCATION

Adult education is what goes on in a household containing teenage children!

If the cost of a college education continues to snowball for many more years, a person can make a profit by remaining ignorant.

I have never let my schooling interfere with my education.                                Mark Twain

Education is too important to be left solely to the educators.

You can lead a boy to college, but you cannot make him think.

Education is a progressive discovery of our ignorance.

## EFFORT

It is hard to fail, but it is worse never to have tried to succeed. In this life we get nothing save by effort.                                Theodore Roosevelt

## EGO

The only thing that can keep on growing without nourishment.

## EGRESS

It is said that Phineas T. Barnum, the famed circus magnate, hung a large sign over one of the exits of his museum, which read, "This way to the egress." Many people in the crowds, eager to see what an egress looked like, passed through the door and found themselves out on the street.

## ELEPHANTS

Why do elephants paint their toe nails purple?
So they can hide in grape vines.
Does it really work?
Have you ever seen an elephant in a grape vine?

Question:  What would you do if an elephant
           sat in front of you in a movie?
Answer:    Miss most of the picture.

Question: How do you sculpture an elephant?

Answer: You take a big block of marble and chip away anything that doesn't look like an elephant.

## EMBARRASSING

Nothing is as embarassing as watching your boss do something you assured him couldn't be done.

## ENCORE

Comedian: "Look here, I do object to going on right after the monkey act."

Manager: "You're right. They may think it's an encore."

## ENCOURAGEMENT

Kind words are like honey — enjoyable and healthful.                    Proverbs 16:24

Anxious hearts are very heavy but a word of encouragement does wonders!

Proverbs 12:25

Encouragement after censure is as the sun after a shower.                         Goethe

Some little word of encouragement may help a work as much as a great effort.

Johnny: "Lawrence is just bashful. Why don't you give him a little encouragement."

Bonnie: "Encouragement? He needs a cheering section!"

## ENDS

Why is it every time you start to make ends meet — somebody comes along and moves the ends?

## ENDURE
What cannot be cured
Must be endured.

## ENERGETIC
The energetic man and his bed are soon parted.

## ENJOYMENT
May we never let the things we can't have, or don't have, or shouldn't have, spoil our enjoyment of the things we do have and can have. As we value our happiness let us not forget it, for one of the greatest lessons in life is learning to be happy without the things we cannot or should not have.

## ENTHUSIASM
Enthusiasm comes from what I concentrate on.

## ERASER
The best eraser in the world is a good night's sleep.

## ERROR
Error always rides the back of truth.

To err is human, but when the eraser wears out ahead of the pencil, you're overdoing it.

The man who makes no mistakes does not usually make anything.

It takes less time to do a thing right than it does to explain why you did it wrong.
                    Henry Wadsworth Longfellow

## ESTATE
Lawyer: "Among other things, your uncle left you over five hundred clocks."

Heir:     "Oh dear! It will take a long time to wind up his estate, won't it?"

## EVE
Eve was the first person who ate herself out of house and home.

Sunday School teacher: Class what do you know about Adam's wife, Eve?
Student: They named Christmas Eve for her.

Weary salesclerk: "Did you ever wonder how many fig leaves Eve tried on before she said, 'I'll have this one'?"

## EXAGGERATE

Tim:     You are beautiful. You are sweet, fine, wonderful. You are everything that's good.
Beverly: Oh, you flatterer, how you exaggerate.
Tim:     Well, that's my story and I'll stick to it.

## EXCELLENT

Every good and excellent thing stands moment by moment on the razor's edge of danger and must be fought for.

## EXCITING

The backslider gets bored with himself; the godly man's life is exciting.

Proverbs 14:14

## EXCUSES

He that is good for making excuses is seldom good for anything else.        Benjamin Franklin

## EXECUTIVE

An executive is a man who can make quick decisions that are right sometimes.

## EXPERIENCE

When I was a boy of fourteen, my father was so ignorant I could hardly stand to have the old man around. But when I got to be twenty-one, I was astonished at how much the old man had learned in seven years.        Mark Twain

Experience is one thing you can't get for nothing.        Oscar Wilde

The name that men give to their mistakes.

Men who leave home to set the world on fire, often come back for more matches.

Experience is the thing you have left when everything else is gone.

Ever notice that about the time you think you're to graduate from the school of experience, somebody thinks up a new course?

An employer interviewing an applicant remarked, "You ask high wages for a man with no experience."
"Well," he replied, "it's so much harder to work when you don't know anything about it."

Experience: The wonderful knowledge that enables you to recognize a mistake when you make it again.

## EXPERT

Question: What is the definition of an expert?
Answer: Someone called in at the last minute to share the blame.

A person who has no business of his own to wreck.

## EXTERMINATOR

Exterminator's office: "We make mouse calls."

## FACE

"Your face would stop a clock."
"And yours would make one run!"

If your face is your fortune . . . you won't have to pay any income tax.

Something we would like to save, especially if we have lost our head.

## FACTS

Get your facts first, and then you can distort them as much as you please.          Mark Twain

What a shame — yes, how stupid! — to decide before knowing the facts!          Proverbs 18:13

## FAIR

None but the brave can afford the fair.

## FAIRNESS

We must be courteous to a man as we are to a picture, which we are willing to give the advantage of a good light.          Emerson

God is more pleased when we are just and fair than when we give Him gifts.          Proverbs 21:3

The Lord demands fairness in every business deal. He established this principle.
          Proverbs 16:11

## FAITHFUL

A faithful employee is as refreshing as a cool day in the hot summertime.          Proverbs 25:13

## FALSE

Question: What do we call the last teeth to appear in the mouth?
Answer:   False.

## FALL

Don't fall in the fire to be saved from the smoke.

## FAME

The ability to die at the right moment.

Fame is proof that people are gullible.
          Ralph Waldo Emerson

## FAMILY

The only thing missing in the American home.

The three stages of modern family life are matrimony, acrimony, and alimony.

A happy family is but an earlier heaven.

Nowadays, a family is a group of people who have keys to the same house.

The average American family consists of 4.1 persons. You have one guess as to who constitutes the .1 person.

## FANS

What makes a baseball stadium cool?
Answer: The fans.

## FAT

He's so fat he can't tell where to bend over and where to sit down. So he has someone hit him with a board and if it knocks the wind out of him, he knows that side is his stomach.

Question: Why are you fat?
Answer: I'm not fat. I just retain flesh.

Question: How did you get so fat?
Answer: I became pregnant and I never gave birth. My baby decided to live in.

Question: You have such a pretty face how come you let your figure go?
Answer: Because . . . as hard as I tried, I couldn't let my face go.

Question: Do you know it's not healthy to be so fat?
Answer: No . . . hum a few bars for me.

Question   How did you get so fat?
Answer:     When I was a kid I got the mumps and it never cleared up.

Question:   Are there any jobs for people as fat as yourself?
Answer:     Yes. A stewardess on the Good Year Blimp.

Those ladies are so fat that it looks like the finals in the Miss Over-active Thyroid Contest.

## FAULTS

However blind a man may be,
Another's faults he's sure to see.

A fault denied is twice committed.

## FEAR

Fear that man who fears not God.

Fear is the tax that conscience pays to guilt.

There's nothing I'm afraid of like scared people.
                       Robert Frost

## FEEL

"How do you feel?"
"I feel just like I look."
"That's too bad."

## FIDELITY

Nothing is more noble, nothing more venerable than fidelity. Faithfulness and truth are the most sacred excellences and endowments of the human mind.                 Cicero

## FIGHTS

Fools start fights everywhere while wise men try to keep peace.             Proverbs 29:8

## FINANCE

Alexander Hamilton originated the put and take system in our national treasury: the taxpayers put it in, and the politicians take it out.          Will Rogers

One-third of the people in the United States promote, while the other two-thirds provide.

Will Rogers

## FINANCE COMPANY

A conspiracy to extend a modest business . . . first established by Black Beard.

## FINISHERS

The world has lots of starters but very few finishers.

## FIRE INSURANCE

Bob: Does your uncle carry life insurance?
R.D.: No, he just carries fire insurance. He knows where he is going.

## FISH

A large water creature that always seems to get away from a man.

A fish gains weight slowly, except the one that got away.

Fish and guests smell at three days old.

Brad: I've eaten beef all my life, and now I'm strong as an ox.
Rich: That's funny. I've eaten fish all my life and I can't swim a stroke.

## FLAGSTONE

Husband put in a flagstone walk from house to street. When he finished he called his wife to come look. "It is terrible, the colors don't match, the stones are crooked." Weary and disappointed he asked: "How is it for length?"

## FLEA

Teacher: The man named Lot was warned to take his wife and flee out of the city, but his wife looked back and was turned to salt.

Student: "What happened to the flea?"

## FLEECE

Sometimes we think the wicked fleece and no man pursueth.

## FLIRT

Sally: I wonder what's wrong with that tall blond guy over there. Just a minute ago he was getting awful friendly, and then all of a sudden he turned pale, walked away, and won't even look at me anymore.

Linda: Maybe he saw me come in. He's my husband.

## FLUID

Man to friend: "You might describe my financial situation as fluid. Which is a sort of nice way of saying I'm going down the drain."

## FLU SEASON

Hoarse and buggy days.

## FOLLY

It is safer to meet a bear robbed of her cubs than a fool caught in his folly.          Proverbs 17:12

## FOOL

After a big night on the town, one man was heard to say, "A fool and his money are some party."

In the mouth of a fool a proverb becomes as useless as a paralyzed leg.

No woman makes a fool out of a man . . . she merely directs the performance.

When two men quarrel there is at least one fool, and the man that interferes makes two.

He who would make a fool of himself will find many to help him.

He who is his own lawyer has a fool for a client.

It's a silly goose that comes to a fox's sermon.

We all know a fool when we see one — but not when we are one.

A fool gets into constant fights. His mouth is his undoing! His words endanger him.

Proverbs 18:6-7

A fool and his money are soon parted.

The best way to convince a fool that he is wrong is to let him have his own way.

Josh Billings

No fools are so troublesome as those who have some wit.          Francois de La Rochfoucauld

## FOOLISH

A foolish man may be known by six things: Anger without cause, speech without profit, change without progress, inquiry without object, putting trust in a stranger, and mistaking foes for friends.

## FOOT

Parents who are afraid to put their foot down usually have children who step on their toes.

Put your foot down where you mean to stand.

## FORGETFUL

"George is so forgetful," the sales manager complained to his secretary. "It's a wonder he can sell anything. I asked him to pick me up some sandwiches on his way back from lunch, and I'm not sure he'll even remember to come back."

Just then the door flew open, and in bounced George. "You'll never guess what happened!" he shouted. "While I was at lunch, I met old man Brown, who hasn't bought anything from us for five years. Well, we got to talking and he gave me this half-million dollar order!"

"See, sighed the sales manager to his secretary, "I told you he'd forget the sandwiches."

## FORK

If you drop a fork it's a sign company is coming . . . if a fork is missing it's a sign company is going.

## FRAGRANCE

It is always wise to stop wishing for things long enough to enjoy the fragrance of those now flowering.

## FRAU

Many a man lives by the sweat of his frau.

## FREE SPEECH

Etta:     "Do you believe in free speech?"
Gretta:  "I certainly do."
Etta:     "Then may I make a long distance call on your telephone?"

Free speech isn't dead in Russia . . . only the speakers.

It is by the goodness of God that in our country we have these three unspeakable precious things: Freedom of speech, freedom of conscience and the prudence never to practice either of them.

Mark Twain

**FREETHINKER**

One who is not married.

**FRIEND**

A friend is one who knows you as you are, understands where you've been, accepts who you've become — and still, gently invites you to grow.

For many years a certain white whale and a tiny herring had been inseparable friends. Wherever the white whale roamed in search of food, the herring was sure to be swimming right along beside him.

One fine spring day the herring turned up off the coast of Norway without his companion. Naturally all the other fish were curious, and an octopus finally asked the herring what happened to his whale friend.

"How should I know?" the herring replied. "Am I my blubber's kipper?"

It's poor friendship that needs to be constantly bought.

Defend me from my friends; I can defend myself from my enemies.

Judge yourself by the friends you form.

Friends are like fiddle strings, they must not be screwed too tight.

True friends are greatest riches.

A man that hath friends must show himself friendly. Bible

Choose your friends with care, that you may have choice friends.

A man dies as often as he loses his friends.

There are "friends" who pretend to be friends, but there is a friend who sticks closer than a brother.                                    Proverbs 18:24

## FROG

In a frog-jumping contest in Calaveras County, California, the entry from the state of Kentucky was named Man-o-Wart.

## FRUGAL

The man walked into the house panting and almost completely exhausted. "What happened, honey?" inquired his wife.

"It's a great new idea I have," he gasped. "I ran all the way home behind the bus and saved 50 cents."

"That wasn't very bright," replied his wife. "Why didn't you run behind a taxi and save $3.00?"

A rather frugal man asked the bank for a loan of one dollar and was told he would have to pay 7 percent interest at the end of the year. For security he offered $60,000 in U.S. bonds. The banker, forseeing a potential depositor, accepted the bonds and gave the man a dollar.

At the end of the year, he was back with a dollar and seven cents to clear up his debt and asked for the return of his bonds. Upon returning the bonds the banker asked, "I don't want to be inquisitive, but since you have all those bonds, why did you have to borrow a dollar?" "Well," said the tightfisted old gent, "I really didn't have to. But do you know of any other way I could get the use of a safety deposit box for seven cents a year?"

## FURROW

A plowman is known by his furrow.

# FUTURE

My interest is in the future because I am going to spend the rest of my life there.

The best thing about the future is that it comes only one day at a time.

The trouble with our times is that the future is not what it used to be.

# GALAXIES

NASA reports galaxies are speeding away from earth at 90,000 miles a second. What do you suppose they know that we don't?"

# GAME WARDEN

"Are you the game warden?" asked a lady over the telephone.

"Yes, I am the game warden," was the reply.

"Oh, I am so glad," said the lady. "Will you please suggest some games for a little party I'm giving for my children?"

# GARDENER

A gardener is known by his garden.

# GASOLINE

The way gas prices are today, anyone who gets less than 15 miles per gallon should have his hood examined.

I had a friend who drove his big new car into a filling station, saying "Fill'er up." After a while, the filling station attendant suggested, "Better shut off your engine. You're gaining on me."

A boy and a girl were out driving one evening. They came to a quiet spot on a country lane, and the car stopped. "Out of gas," said the boy.

The girl opened her purse and pulled out a bottle.

"Wow!" said the boy. "A bottle . . . what is it?"

"Gasoline," said the girl.

## GENERATION

Our generation never got a break. When we were young they taught us to respect our elders. Now that we're older, they tell us to listen to the youth of the country.

The older generation thought nothing of getting up at five every morning — and the younger generation doesn't think much of it either.

## GENTLEMAN

A gentleman is one who never hurts anyone's feelings unintentionally.

Clowns are always best in their own company, but gentlemen are best everywhere.

Someone you don't know very well.

## GEOMETRY

Geometry is easy as $\pi$.

## GETTING STARTED

He has half the deed done, who has made a beginning.

## GIVE

The hardest thing to give is in.

It is better to give than to lend, and it costs about the same.

However much a man gives, there is more that he withholds.

## GIFT
Another name for trade.

## GIRLS
I never expected to see the day when girls would get sunburned in the places they do now.
Will Rogers

A girl is innocence playing in the mud, beauty standing on its head, and motherhood dragging a doll by the foot.

When a boy breaks a date, he usually has to. When a girl breaks a date, she usually has two.

## GLASS EYE
Christy: That lady has a glass eye.
Lisa: How did you find that out?
Christy: Well, it just came out in the conversation.

## GLOOMY
When a man is gloomy, everything seems to go wrong; when he is cheerful, everything seems right!
Proverbs 15:15

## GLUTTON
One who digs his grave with his teeth.

## GNU

Mama Gnu was waiting for Papa Gnu as he came home for dinner one evening. "Our little boy was very bad today," she declared. "I want you to punish him."

"Oh no," said Papa Gnu. "I won't punish him. You'll have to learn to paddle your own gnu."

## GODLINESS

Godly men are growing a tree that bears life-giving fruit, and all who win souls are wise.

Proverbs 11:30

## GOLF

Man to friend: "After three sets of clubs and ten years of lessons, I'm finally getting some fun out of golf. I quit."

Wife to husband at front door carrying golf clubs: "You don't have to go all the way to the golf course for a hole in one. There's one in the roof, one in the screen door, and one in the . . ."

Golf is a lot of walking, broken up by disappointment and bad arithmetic.

By the time you're old enough to afford losing golf balls, you're not hitting them that far.

Wife at 2 a.m. "Where have you been?"
Husband: "Playing golf."
Wife: "After dark?"
Husband: "Yes, we were using night clubs."

Many a man who doesn't play golf can't give it up.

## GOLF CLUB

Another name for a shovel.

## GOOD-BY

Something that money says.

## GOOD NEWS

Good news from far away is like cold water to the thirsty.

## GOSSIP

Fire goes out for lack of fuel, and tensions disappear when gossip stops.          Proverbs 26:20

An evil man sows strife; gossip separates the best of friends.          Proverbs 16:28

A gossip goes around spreading rumors, while a trustworthy man tries to quiet them.
Proverbs 11:13

Don't tell your secrets to a gossip unless you want them broadcast to the world.
Proverbs 20:19

Gossip is a dainty morsel eaten with great relish.
Proverbs 26:22

Question:   What do they call someone who puts who and who together and gets wow!

Answer:     A gossip.

He has ears like steam shovels . . . they're always picking up dirt.

Gossip that comes over the grapevine is usually sour.

"Now listen, did you tell Sara that what you said was in strict confidence?"

"Oh no; I didn't want her to think it was important enough to repeat."

## GOVERNMENT

A large plant that needs more pruning and less grafting.

Most people would be glad to tend their own business if the government would give it back.

We all work for the government but the politician is wise. He gets paid for it.

Measuring big government by the magnitude of a billion:

1 billion seconds ago — the bombing of Pearl Harbor.

1 billion minutes ago — Christ was living on earth.

1 billion hours ago — man had not yet appeared on earth, but

1 billion dollars ago — that was only yesterday.

It's becoming more and more difficult to support the government in the style to which it has become accustomed.

## GRADE

Little Charlie came home with an O on his homework. Naturally, his mother wanted to know why he got an O. "Charlie," she said, "Why is there an O on this paper?"

"That's no O," said Charlie. "The teacher ran out of stars and gave me a moon!"

## GRANDCHILDREN

"Have I told you about my grandchildren?"

"No, and I thank you very much."

## GRAPE

Question:   What's purple and 5000 miles long?

Answer      The Grape Wall of China.

## GRAVE

A grave, wherever found, preaches a short and pithy sermon to the soul.    Nathaniel Hawthorne

The only difference between a rut and a grave is the dimensions. Ellen Glasgow

## GREATNESS

In admiring greatness we rise to its level.

## GREMLIN

An elf-made man.

## GRIPING

Man who beef too much find himself in stew.

## GROW

You grow up the day you have your first real laugh — at yourself. Ethel Barrymore

## GRUDGE

No matter how much you nurse a grudge it won't get better.

## GUEST

A constant guest is never welcome.

Fish and guests smell at three days old.

Unbidden guests are welcome when they are gone.

## GUIDE

A fishing party was hopelessly lost in the deep woods. "I thought you were the best guide in Minnesota," said one man.

"I am," replied the guide, "but I think we're in Canada now."

## GUILTY

The guilty catch themselves.

## GUTTER

Then there was the sanitation worker who got fired because he couldn't keep his mind in the gutter.

"He's a great detective . . . he's always got his ear to the ground. In fact, he's always in the gutter."

## HAIRDO

We're constantly amazed at these young things with their fancy hairdos and skin tight pants. And the girls are even worse.

## HALF-TRUTH

Beware of a half-truth; it may be the wrong half.

## HALOS

Bent Halos Repaired Here.

## HANDS

Many hands make light work:
this is clear.
Many hands make slight work:
this I fear.

## HANGERS

Oh, what a tangled web we weave, when first we drop a bunch of clothes hangers.

## HAPPINESS

Happiness is the art of making a bouquet of those flowers within reach.

Happiness is like perfume: spray it on others and you are bound to get some on yourself.

All happy families resemble one another; every unhappy family is unhappy in its own fashion.

Tolstoi

It is no sillier for the rich to think the poor are happy than for the poor to think the rich are.

Happiness is no laughing matter.

It is pretty hard to tell what does bring happiness: poverty and wealth have both failed.

Pleasant sights and good reports give happiness and health.

Proverbs 15:30

## HAPPY-GO-LUCKY

Being happy-go-lucky around a person whose heart is heavy is as bad as stealing his jacket in cold weather, or rubbing salt in his wounds.

Proverbs 25:20

## HARDWORK

Work hard and become a leader; be lazy and never succeed.                   Proverbs 12:24

Hard work means prosperity; only a fool idles away his time.                   Proverbs 12:11

## HASTE

He who pours water hastily into a bottle spills more than he saves.

Hasty climbers have sudden falls.

Make haste slowly.

Though I am always in haste, I am never in a hurry.                   John Wesley

Marry in haste, and you'll never have any leisure to repent in.

Do not be in a desperate hurry, or you will get into trouble, or at least fail in your endeavors. The Chinese say that "a hasty man drinks his tea with a form."

## HATE

To hate fatigues.

I shall never permit myself to stoop so low as to hate any man.                   Booker T. Washington

A man with hate in his heart may sound pleasant enough, but don't believe him; for he is cursing you in his heart. Though he pretends to be so kind, his hatred will finally come to light for all to see.                                     Proverbs 26:24-26

## HEADWAITER

A tyrant without ears or eyes dressed in a tuxedo.

## HEAR

Don't see all you see, and don't hear all you hear.

## HEART

Two things are bad for the heart — running up stairs and running down people.

Brave hearts are tender hearts.

The great man is he who does not lose his child's heart.

## HELL

The road to Hell is paved with good intentions.
                                          Karl Marx

The wicked work harder to reach hell than the righteous to reach heaven.          Josh Billings

If there is no hell, a good many preachers are obtaining money under false pretenses.
                                     William A. Sunday

Hell is truth seen too late — duty neglected in its season.

A motorist was picked up unconscious after a smash, and was being carried to a nearby filling station. Upon opening his eyes en route, he began to kick and struggle desperately to get away. Afterwards he explained that the first thing he saw was a "Shell" sign, and somebody was standing in front of the "S!"

"There will be weeping, wailing and gnashing of teeth among the wicked who pass on to the next world."
"What about those who haven't got any teeth?"
"Teeth will be provided."

## HEN
If you would have a hen lay, you must bear with her cackling.

## HESITATE
She who hesitates is lost; so is the man who doesn't.

## HICCUPS
We've just heard about a glass blower who was suddenly overcome by hiccups. He turned out a thousand percolator caps before help came.

## HIGH HORSE
Nothing is as hard to do gracefully as getting down off your high horse.

## HIPPIE
A hippie lived in a room with just one chair and a cot for furniture. One night a friend dropped in, and spying two magazines lying in the middle of the floor asked, "Whadja do, man, hire an interior decorator?"

A fellow noticed a flower-bedecked, flowing-haired hippie walking down the street with a cigar box under his arm so he stopped him and asked, "How much are your cigars?"

"I'm not selling cigars," came the answer. "I'm moving."

## HITLER

A very naziating man.

Adolph Hitler was an avid believer in astrology and consulted with his special astrologist before making any decisions.

One day in consulting with him, Hitler asked, "On what day will I die?"

"You will die on a Jewish holiday," replied the astrologist.

"How can you be so sure of that?" asked Hitler.

"Any day you die will be a Jewish holiday," replied the astrologist.

## HOMESICK

"Honest, weren't you ever homesick?"

"Not me, I never stay there long enough."

## HONESTY

Honesty pays, but it don't seem to pay enough to suit some people.

A little, gained honestly, is better than great wealth gotten by dishonest means.

Proverbs 16:8

It pays to be honest, but it's slow pay.

Lies will get any man into trouble, but honesty is its own defense.　　　Proverbs 12:13

## HONOR

The louder he talked of his honor, the faster we counted our spoons.　　　Ralph Waldo Emerson

## HOPE

Those who hope for no other life are dead even in this.         Johann Wolfgang von Goethe

## HORSE

He that can travel well afoot keeps a good horse.         Franklin

## HORSE SENSE

Question:   What is another name for stable thinking.

Answer:     Horse sense.

## HOUSE

Every girl can keep house better than her mother till she tries.

The crown of the house is Godliness. The beauty of the house is order. The glory of the house is hospitality. The blessing of the house is love.

When are houses like books?
When they have stories in them.

## HOSPITALITY

Don't open your door and darken your countenance.

Behave towards everyone as if receiving a great guest.

## HOT DOG

The Hot Dog is the noblest of all dogs because it feeds the hand that bites it.

## HOT-HEADED

Hot-heads make their brains bubble over.

Don't be hot-headed and rush to court! You may start something you can't finish and go down before your neighbor in shameful defeat. So discuss the matter with him privately. Don't tell anyone else, lest he accuse you of slander and you can't withdraw what you said.    Proverbs 25:8-10

## HUGGING

Buck: Did you ever wonder why there are so many more auto wrecks than railway accidents?

Bill: Did you ever hear of the fireman hugging the engineer?

## HUMBLE

Better poor and humble than proud and rich.
Proverbs 16:19

## HUMORIST

Will Rogers once said it's no big deal being a humorist when you have the whole government working for you.

A person who originates old jokes.

## HUSBAND

A man of few words.

An archaeologist is the best husband any woman can have: the older she gets, the more interested he is in her.    Agatha Christie

One good husband is worth two good wives; for the scarcer things are, the more they are valued.

## HYPOCRISY

A hypocrite is a fellow who isn't himself on Sundays.

## ICICLE

A hunter was out in the forest. It was late in the day and getting colder. A bear appeared. The hunter grabbed his gun — there was no ammunition left! He wiped the sweat off his brow and put it in the gun — it shot out as an icicle and pierced the head of the bear and the bear died of water on the brain!

## IDEAS

Many ideas grow better when transplanted into another mind than in the one where they sprung up.                                Oliver Wendell Holmes

Ideas are very much like children — our own are very wonderful.

"I've got an idea."
"Be kind to it. It's a long way from home."

## IDIOT

My wife thinks she's changed. She's always talking about what an idiot she used to be.

"When I was a child I used to bite my fingernails; and the doctor told me if I didn't quit it I'd grow up to be an idiot."
"And you couldn't stop, huh?"

Our town was too small to have a village idiot so we all took turns.

## IDOLATRY

The idol is the measure of the worshiper.
                                James Russell Lowell

## IGNORAMUS

It's difficult to define the word, "ignoramus," unless one has studied himself pretty carefully.

## IMAGE

Mother: The baby is the image of his father.
Neighbor: What do you care, so long as he is healthy.

## IMPASSABLE

A wet football.

## IMPERFECTIONS

'Tis a mark of great perfection to bear with the imperfections of others.

## IMPOSSIBILITY

The difficult is that which can be done immediately; the impossible that which takes a little longer.

## IMPROVE

Of all the awkward people in your house there is only one whom you can improve very much.

People seldom improve when they have no other model but themselves to copy after.

## INCOME TAX

An income tax return is like a girdle. If you put the wrong figure in it, you're apt to get pinched.

## INDEPENDENCE

It is not the greatness of a man's means that makes him independent, so much as the smallness of his wants.

## INDIAN

Clerk: This jug was made by a real Indian.
Elmer: But it says here it's made in Cleveland, Ohio.
Clerk: Well, didn't you ever hear of the Cleveland Indians?

## INDISTINCT

Question: Where do people put dirty dishes?
Answer: Indistinct.

## INFLATION

Two can still live as cheaply as one . . . if one doesn't show up.

Inflation is when the buck doesn't stop anywhere.

Inflation marches on, making it possible for people in all walks of life to live in more expensive neighborhoods without ever moving.

I have it all figured out. If I continue saving at the present rate, I'll retire owing $50,000.

The way prices keep going up, the next thing we know they'll have the bargain basement on the third floor.

One good thing about inflation is that it's practically impossible for a youngster to get sick on a 5-cent candy bar.

## INFERIORITY

Then there was the teen whose spirit was so low that he told his buddy, "The only way I can feel superior is by seeing that my inferiority complex is bigger than anyone else's."

No one can make you feel inferior without your consent.
Eleanor Roosevelt

We must interpret a bad temper as a sign of inferiority.
Alfred Adler

No man likes to have his intelligence or good faith questioned, especially if he has doubts about it himself.
Henry Brooks Adams

## INFIDELITY

The nurse of infidelity is sensuality.

## INGRATITUDE

How sharper than a serpent's tooth it is
To have a thankless child!

William Shakespeare

A proud man is seldom a grateful man, for he never thinks he gets as much as he deserves.

Henry Ward Beecher

My brother was sort of odd. I remember once on his birthday he fell down a dry well. So we lowered his birthday cake to him. He didn't even tug on the rope to say thanks.

## IN-LAWS

Advice squad.

Men speak of their in-laws as if their wives didn't have any.

## INSANE ASYLUM

A home for old joke book writers.

## INSECURE

Mother of small boy to child psychiatrist: "Well, I don't know whether or not he feels insecure, but everybody else in the neighborhood certainly does!"

## INSTALLMENT BUYING

A system that makes the months shorter and the years longer.

## INSTRUMENT

One of the most difficult instruments to play well is second fiddle.

## INSULT

There are two insults no human being will endure: that he has no sense of humor, and that he has never known trouble.

Sinclair Lewis

"One of your guests insulted me!"
"Only one?"

"I hear you were out dining in a swell home last night?"
"Yes, just as we sat down at the table, the host insulted me. I got so mad that I left right after the supper."

## INTERFERING

Yanking a dog's ear is no more foolish than interfering in an argument that isn't any of your business.                    Proverbs 26:17

## INTELLIGENT

The intelligent man is always open to new ideas. In fact, he looks for them.

Proverbs 18:15

## I.Q.

He had an extremely high I.Q. when he was five . . . too bad he grew out of it.

## IRRITATION

Women are more irritable than men, the reason being that men are more irritating.

## INVALID

Christy: I was an invalid once.
Lisa:    You were? When was that?
Christy: When I was a baby. I couldn't walk until I was a year old.

## INVEST

Wondering where to invest? Invest some time in your family . . . the dividends are great.

## INVOLVED

Only the person involved can know his own bitterness or joy — no one else can really share it.

Proverbs 14:10

## JAYWALKING

For that run-down feeling — try jaywalking.

## JEALOUSY

Jealousy is more dangerous and cruel than anger.               Proverbs 12:12

There is more self-love than love in jealousy.
              Francois de La Rochefoucauld

The jealous man poisons his own banquet, and then eats it.

And oft, my jealousy shapes faults that are not.
              William Shakespeare

Lots of people know a good thing the minute the other fellow sees it first.

There is never jealousy where there is not strong regard.               Washington Irving

## JEST

He that would jest must take a jest,
Else to let it alone were best.

When the jest is at its best,
'Twill be well to let it rest.

A jest driven too far brings home hate.

The jest loses its point when he who makes it is the first to laugh.

Judge of a jest when you have done laughing.

Many a true word is spoken in jest.

## JOAN OF ARC

A little boy, just back from Sunday School, asked his father if Noah had a wife.

"All the time, questions, questions, questions," replied the father. "Of course he did, Joan of Arc."

## J.O.B.

Many people nowadays have a B.A., M.A., or Ph.D. — but not always a J.O.B.

## JOINT

No glue will hold when the joint is bad.

## JOURNALISM

Journalists do not live by words alone, although sometimes they have to eat them.

Adlai E. Stevenson

A journalist is a grumbler, a censurer, a giver of advice, a regent of sovereigns, a tutor of nations. Four hostile newspapers are more to be feared than a thousand bayonets.    Napoleon Bonaparte

## JUDGMENT

Everyone complains of the badness of his memory, but nobody of his judgment.

Francois de La Rochefoucauld

You shall judge of a man by his foes as well as by his friends.

Snap judgment has a way of coming unfastened.

## JUSTICE

Justice is the first virtue of those who command, and stops the complaints of those who obey.

Children are innocent and love justice, while most adults are wicked and prefer mercy.

Gilbert K. Chesterton

Justice tempered with too much mercy becomes injustice.

You should defend those who cannot help themselves. Yes, speak up for the poor and needy and see that they get justice.

Proverbs 31:8,9

## KIDS

Children would all be brought up perfectly if families would just swap kids. Everyone knows what ought to be done with the neighbor's kids.

One nice thing about kids is that they don't keep telling you boring stories about the clever things their parents said.

## KIND

Speak kind words and you will hear kind echoes.

He is kind to himself who is kind to his wife.

A gift with a kind word is a double gift.

## KINDNESS

Kindness is loving people more than they deserve.

Kindness goes a long way lots of times when it ought to stay at home.

He that has done you a kindness will be more ready to do you another than he whom you yourself have obliged.          Benjamin Franklin

## KING

Wise kings generally have wise counselors; and he must be a wise man himself who is capable of distinguishing one.          Diogenes

The lion went up to the rhinoceros and asked, "Who is the king of the jungle?"

"You are, O lion," came the answer.

The lion went up to the hippopotamus and asked, "Who is the king of the jungle?"

The hippo said, "You are, O lion."

The lion went up to the elephant and asked, "Who is the king of the jungle?"

For an answer the elephant seized the lion with his trunk, threw him high in the air, caught him on the way down, and slammed him hard against a tree.

The lion arose, half dazed, shook himself, and said weakly, "Just because you don't know the right answer, you don't have to get sore."

## KLEPTOMANIA

The thing about kleptomania is, if you've got it, you can always take something for it.

## KNOWLEDGE

I am not young enough to know everything.

If a little knowledge is dangerous, where is the man who has so much as to be out of danger?

He who knows but little shares it often.

He who knows but little tells it quickly.

Knowledge is a treasure, but practice is the key to it.

He who carves the Buddha never worships him.

He who knows more speaks least.

I keep six honest serving-men
(They taught me all I knew);
Their names are What and Why and When
And How and Where and Who.

Rudyard Kipling

All wish to possess knowledge, but few, comparatively speaking, are willing to pay the price.

He who knows not, and knows not that he knows not, is a fool. Shun him.

He who knows not, and knows that he knows not is simple. Teach him.

He knows so little and knows it fluently.

## LADY KILLER

Guy: I'm a lady killer.
Gal:  Yeah, they take one look at you and drop dead.

## LANGUAGE

Language is the dress of thought.

Samuel Johnson

Because everyone uses language to talk, everyone thinks he can talk about language.

Johann Wolfgang von Goethe

## LAS VEGAS

A friend of ours says he never wants to see Las Vegas again. His luck was so bad he lost his shirt in a coin laundry.

## LAUGHTER

Those who bring sunshine to the lives of others cannot keep it from themselves.

Laughter is the tonic, the relief, the surcease for pain.  Charlie Chaplin

The young man who has not wept is a savage, and the old man who will not laugh is a fool.

George Santayana

A hearty laugh gives one a dry cleaning, while a good cry is a wet wash.

A man isn't poor if he can still laugh.

Laughter is the sun that drives winter from the human face.                    Victor Hugo

I can usually judge a fellow by what he laughs at.

He who has the courage to laugh is almost as much master of the world as he who is ready to die.

Laughter cannot mask a heavy heart. When the laughter ends, the grief remains.
                                          Proverbs 14:13

A laugh is worth a hundred groans in any market.

He who laughs — lasts.

Laughter — The annoying sound the other person makes when you get what you didn't have coming.

Belly laugh: Mirthquake.

## LAWN
Any child who is anxious to mow the lawn is too young to do it.

## LAWYERS
Two lawyers were opposing each other for political office. "Did you tell Jake down at the barbershop that I'm a thieving, lying shyster?" asked one. "No," replied the other, "I don't know how he found out."

My son, a lawyer, was approached by his friend, a priest, who wanted a will drawn up. When the work was completed and ready to be mailed, my son couldn't resist inserting this note: "Thy Will Be Done."

## LAZINESS

The mother of invention.

## LEADERSHIP

The final test of a leader is that he leaves behind him in other men the conviction and the will to carry on.                    Walter Lippmann

If the blind lead the blind, both shall fall into the ditch.                    Matthew 15:14, KJV

Leadership: The art of getting someone else to do something you want done because he wants to do it.                    Dwight D. Eisenhower

Without wise leadership, a nation is in trouble; but with good counselors there is safety.
                    Proverbs 11:14

## LEFTOVERS

The lady said to the waitress "May I have a bag to carry leftovers to my dog?"
Her 6-year-old said: "Oh, Mother, are we going to get a dog?"

## LEND

If you want to lose a troublesome visitor, lend him money.

## LEVEE

One leg of a pair of levis.

## LIBBER

Did you hear about the little libber down the block — she insists that her Halloween pumpkin is a jill-o-lantern.

# LIBRARY

A library is a place where the dead live.

In college library: "Quiet — don't disturb the strain of thought."

# LIES

A lie travels round the world while truth is putting on her boots.  C.H. Spurgeon

Liars should have good memories.

Oh, what a tangled web we weave
One lie needs seven to wait upon it.

If you tell a big enough lie and tell it frequently enough, it will be believed.  Hitler

Lies need a great deal of killing.

Telling lies about someone is as harmful as hitting him with an axe, or wounding him with a sword, or shooting him with a sharp arrow.

Gal: You're very handsome.
Guy: Gee. I wish I could say something nice about you.
Gal: You could if you lied as well as I did.

Joe: How can you lie like that and look me in the face?
Moe: I'm getting used to your face.

# LIFESAVER

The fellow who invented the lifesaver really made a mint.

# LIGHTNING

Lightning never strikes twice in the same place . . . it doesn't have to.

## LISTEN

It is a kingly act to listen to reason.

Before you decide
Hear the other side.

A good listener is a silent flatterer.

## LITERATURE

Our high respect for a well-read man is praise enough of literature.          Ralph Waldo Emerson

## LIVE

Let us endeavor so to live that when we come to die even the undertaker will be sorry.

Mark Twain

## LOAFED

It is better to have loafed and lost than never to have loafed at all.          James Thurber

## LOANS

Sign in a loan company office. "We serve the man who has everything but hasn't paid for it."

Loan Department officer bidding farewell to disappointed couple: "Sorry, but I hope you'll try us again sometime when you don't need it quite so badly."

It is risky to make loans to strangers.

Proverbs 20:16

John:  Lend me fifty.
Jack:  I have only forty.
John:  Well, then let me have the forty and you can owe me the ten.

## LONELINESS

I was never less alone than when by myself.

Edward Gibbon

Language has created the word loneliness to express the pain of being alone, and the word solitude to express the glory of being alone.

Paul Tillich

The whole conviction of my life now rests upon the belief that loneliness, far from being a rare and curious phenomenon, peculiar to myself and to a few other solitary men, is the central and inevitable fact of human existence.          Thomas Wolfe

There are some people who not only keep you from being lonely, but make you wish you were.

## LOOPHOLE

On visiting a seriously ill lawyer in the hospital, his friend found him sitting up in bed, frantically leafing through the Bible.

"What are you doing?" asked the friend.

"Looking for loopholes," replied the lawyer.

## LOST AND FOUND

Bill:   I just found this nice new penknife on the sidewalk.

Dad:   Are you sure it was lost?

Bill:   I'm very sure. I saw the man looking for it.

## LOVE

A man usually falls in love with the girl who asks the kind of questions he is able to answer.

Love: the delusion that one woman differs from another.          H.L. Mencken

He that falls in love with himself will have no rivals.          Benjamin Franklin

A little foolishness and a lot of curiosity.

Love is blind — and marriage is an eye-opener.

Guy: Margie, I love you! I love you Margie!

Gal: In the first place, you don't love me; and in the second place, my name isn't Margie.

Becky: Do you love me with all your heart and soul?

Dave: Uh-huh.

Becky: Do you think I'm the most beautiful girl in the world?

Dave: Uh-huh.

Becky: Do you think my lips are like rose petals?

Dave: Uh-huh.

Becky: Oh, you say the most beautiful things.

John: I can't seem to get anywhere with Jan.

Jack: What happened?

John: I told her I was knee-deep in love with her.

Jack: What was her reaction?

John: She promised to put me on her wading list.

Linda: Do you really love me, or do you just think you do?

Jack: Honey, I really love you . . . I haven't done any thinking yet.

Better to have loved a short man than never to have loved a tall.

## LUCK

I believe in luck: how else can you explain the success of those you dislike?     Jean Cocteau

Depend on the rabbit's foot if you will, but remember it didn't work for the rabbit.

R.E. Shay

I am a great believer in luck and I find the harder I work, the more I have of it.

Good luck is often bad luck in disguise.

## LYING

The liar's punishment is not in the least that he is not believed, but that he cannot believe anyone else.                              George Bernard Shaw

A man who is caught lying to his neighbor and says, "I was just fooling," is like a madman throwing around firebrands, arrows, and death!
                              Proverbs 26:18-19

## MAHARAJA

The maharaja of an Indian province decreed a ban on hunting wildlife, and soon the country was overrun with man-eating animals. When the people could stand it no longer, they gave the maharaja the heave-ho. This may be the first time in history when the reign was called on account of game.

## MAN

All that I care to know is that a man is a human being — that is enough for me; he can't be any worse.                              Mark Twain

## MANSLAUGHTER

A man charged with murder bribed a friend on the jury to hold out for a verdict of manslaughter. The jury was out for a long period of time, but at last brought in a verdict of manslaughter.

Upon visiting the prisoner the following week, the friend was thanked. "You must have had a tough time getting them to vote for manslaughter."

"Tough is right," replied the friend. "The other eleven wanted to acquit you."

## MARBLEHEAD

"In Massachusetts they named a town after you."
"What is it?"
"Marblehead."

## MARRIAGE

Keep your eyes wide open before marriage — half shut afterwards.

Marriages may be made in heaven, but man is responsible for the maintenance work.

If a child of God marries a child of the devil, said child of God is sure to have some trouble with his father-in-law.

Marriages are made in heaven, but they are lived on earth.

Marriage is like the army . . . everyone complains, but you'd be surprised at how many re-enlist.

Son: How much does it cost to get married, Dad?
Dad: I don't know. I'm still paying on it.

Modern marriage is like a cafeteria. A woman grabs what she wants and pays for it later.

"What do you think of trial marriages?"
"I must be frank . . . all marriages are trial marriages."

"Can you take dictation?"
"No, I've never been married."

She calls her husband "Henry." He's the eighth.

Jan:  I want to congratulate you. This is one of
      the happiest days of your life.
Barb: But I'm not getting married until
      tomorrow.
Jan:  That's why I say today is one of your
      happiest days.

Jay:  I have half a mind to get married.
Bufe: That's all you need.

Women are fools to marry men. On the other
hand, what else is there to marry?

I think I am losing my mind but my husband told
me it's impossible because he says I never had one.

"The man who married my mother got a prize."
"What was it?"

## MARTYR

It is the cause and not merely the death that
makes the martyr.          Napoleon Bonaparte

To an unjust government a martyr is more
dangerous than a rebel.

## MATTERHORN

From a schoolboy's exam paper: Matterhorn
was a horn blown by the ancients when anything
was the matter.

## MAYFLOWER

"My folks came over on the Mayflower."

"Don't feel bad about it. We can't all be born here."

## MAXIM

Pithy sentences are like sharp nails which force truth upon our memory.       Denis Diderot

All maxims have their antagonist maxims; proverbs should be sold in pairs, a single one being but a half truth.       William Matthews

All the good maxims have been written. It only remains to put them into practice.

A good maxim is never out of season.

## MEDICAL STUDENT

A medical student was asked how much of a certain drug should be administered to a patient. The young man replied, "Five grains."

A minute later he raised his hand. "Professor," he said, "I would like to change my answer to that question."

The professor looked at his watch and replied, "Never mind. Your patient has been dead for forty seconds."

## MEDITATION

A fool is always meditating how he shall begin his life; a wise man, how he shall end it.

## MERCY

He reminds me of the man who murdered both his parents, and then when sentence was about to be pronounced, pleaded for mercy on the grounds that he was an orphan.       Lincoln

## MEMOIRS

There's nothing a man can do to improve himself so much as writing his memoirs.

## MEMORY

If you have to keep reminding yourself of a thing, perhaps it isn't so.　　　Christopher Morley

Those who cannot remember the past are condemned to repeat it.

Memory is the cabinet of imagination, the treasure of reason, the registry of conscience, and the council chamber of thought.

A liar should have a good memory.

One of the stimuli that keeps a chaperone awake is memory.

## MENTAL BLOCK

A street on which several psychiatrists live.

## MENU

American Tourist in France: "Waiter, bring me some of this — see, here on the menu."

Waiter: "Madam, the orchestra is playing it now."

## MIDGET

During the days of the Salem, Massachusetts, witch hunts, a midget was imprisoned for fortune-telling. She later escaped from jail, and the headline in the local newspaper read: SMALL MEDIUM AT LARGE.

## MILLIONAIRE

A billionaire after taxes.

## MIND

I have a prodigious quantity of mind; it takes me as much as a week sometimes to make it up.

Mark Twain

The mind is like the stomach. It is not how much you put into it that counts, but how much it digests.

From a wise mind comes careful and persuasive speech.                        Proverbs 16:23

## MINUTES
Take care of the minutes; the hours will take care of themselves.

## MIRROR
"I practice smiling in front of a mirror."
"I bet it works . . . I can't keep from laughing myself."

## MIRTH
A man without mirth is like a wagon without springs.

## MISERY
If misery loves company, misery has company enough.                        Henry David Thoreau

## MISFORTUNE
Misfortune comes on horseback, and goes away on foot.

The misfortunes hardest to bear are those which never come.

## MISTAKE
What a doctor buries.

A well-adjusted person is one who makes the same mistake twice without getting nervous.

The great mistake — giving up.

## MOCKER
A mocker stays away from wise men because he hates to be scolded.                        Proverbs 15:12

A wise man is hungry for truth, while the mocker feeds on trash.　　　Proverbs 15:14

Punish a mocker and others will learn from his example. Reprove a wise man and he will be the wiser.　　　Proverbs 19:25

Throw out the mocker, and you will be rid of tension, fighting, and quarrels.　　　Proverbs 22:10

## MODESTY

The art of encouraging others to find out for themselves how important you are.

## MOONSHINE

The prosecution and defense had both presented their final arguments in a case involving a Kentucky moonshiner.

The judge turned to the jury and asked: "Before giving you your instructions, do any of you have any questions?"

"Yes, Your Honor," replied one of the jurors. "Did the defendant boil the malt one or two hours, does he cool it quickly, and at what point does he add the yeast?"

## MONEY

. . . that when someone says, "It's only money," it's usually your money he's talking about.

Money used to talk, then it whispered. Now it just sneaks off.

Make all you can, save all you can, give all you can.　　　John Wesley

When I have any money I get rid of it as quickly as possible, lest it find a way into my heart.
　　　John Wesley

Most money is tainted. Taint yours and taint mine.

The easiest way to teach children the value of money is to borrow some from them.

Money has wings and most of us see only the tail feathers.

To get money is difficult, to keep it more difficult, but to spend it wisely most difficult of all.

If you want to know what a dollar is worth, try to borrow one.

Dishonest money brings grief to all the family, but hating bribes brings happiness.

Proverbs 15:27

Mom's yearning capacity is greater than Dad's earning capacity.

There's something bigger than money . . . bills.

Money brings only misery. But with money you can afford it.

## MONUMENT
Deeds, not stones, are the true monuments of the great.

## MORNING
I hate mornings . . . they're so early.

## MORTGAGE
A small house is better than a large mortgage.

## MOSQUITO
The mosquito has no preference, he bites folks fat or thin.
But the welt that he raises, itches like blazes.
And that's where "the rub" comes in.

## MOTHER'S DAY

Mother's Day brings back memories of maternal advice and admonition. Picture the scene with these famous offspring:

Alexander the Great's mother: "How many times do I have to tell you — you can't have everything you want in this world!"

Franz Schubert's mother: "Take my advice, son. Never start anything you can't finish."

Achilles' mother: "Stop imagining things. There's nothing wrong with your heel."

Madame de Pompadour's mother: "For heaven's sake, child, do something about your hair!"

Sigmund Freud's mother: "Stop pestering me! I've told you a hundred times the stork brought you!"

## MOTIVE

We can justify our every deed but God looks at our motives.                    Proverbs 21:2

## MOUNTAINS

You must scale the mountains if you would view the plain. Chinese proverb

## MOUSE

Teacher: Robert Burns wrote "To a Field Mouse."

Student: I'll bet he didn't get an answer.

## MULE

Cutting off a mule's ear won't make him a horse.

## MUZZLED

A bear never knows until he is muzzled how many people are not afraid of him.

## NAIL

He is the kind of guy that hits the nail on the hand every time.

## NARROW

A narrow mind and a wide mouth usually go together.

## NEARSIGHTED

Jack: I'm so nearsighted I nearly worked myself to death.

Elmer: What's being nearsighted got to do with working yourself to death?

Jack: I couldn't tell whether the boss was watching me or not, so I had to work all the time.

## NEEDS

He who buys what he needs not, sells what he needs.

## NEIGHBOR

Don't visit your neighbor too often, or you will outwear your welcome!     Proverbs 25:17

Don't expect your neighbor to be better than your neighbor's neighbor.

## NEUROTIC

Now there's a list of the ten most neurotic people. It's called "The Best-Stressed List."

My fourth husband is more neurotic than my third husband. I should have never left my third husband

## NEWS

Ill news flies fast enough.

## NICKEL

If a nickel knew what it is worth today, it would feel like two cents.

About all you can get with a nickel these days is heads or tails.

## NIGHT

Late-staying guest: "Well, good night. I hope I have not kept you up too late."

Yawning Host: "Not at all. We would have been getting up soon, anyway."

## NOAH

As Noah remarked while the animals were boarding the Ark, "Now I've herd everything."

## NONSENSE

A little nonsense now and then,
Is relished by the wisest men.

## NOSE

Cleopatra's nose: had it been shorter, the whole aspect of the world would have been altered.

Pascal

"So you had an operation on your nose?"

"Yes, it was getting so I could hardly talk through it."

## NUDITY

Phyllis Diller says there's so much nudity in films that this year's Oscar for clothing design will probably go to a dermatologist.

## OARS

The fellow who's busy pulling on the oars hasn't got time to rock the boat.

## OBEDIENCE

He that hath learned to obey will know how to command.

There are two kinds of men who never amount to much: those who cannot do what they are told, and those who can do nothing else.

One of the first things one notices in a backward country is that children are still obeying their parents.

## OBSCENE

What is this world coming to? I hear they just arrested a fellow who talks dirty to plants. Caught him making an obscene fern call!

## OBSTACLE

An obstacle is often an unrecognized opportunity.

## OFFENSE

It is harder to win back the friendship of an offended brother than to capture a fortified city. His anger shuts you out like iron bars.   Proverbs 18:29

## OLD AGE

More people would live to a ripe old age if they weren't too busy providing for it.

Young man: Why did you live to be the age of 115?
Old man:     Mainly because I was born in 1861.

## OLD-TIMER

One who remembers when people who wore blue jeans worked.

You're an old-timer if you remember when the only babes politicians kissed were those in their mother's arms.

You are an old-timer if you remember when a babysitter was called Mother.

## ONE-TRACK

Most people operate on a one-track mind of two rails — "ME" and "I".

## OPERETTA

Question:  What is an operetta?
Answer:  A girl who works for the telephone
              company.

## OPPORTUNITY

Opportunities always look bigger going than coming.

Lots of people know a good thing the minute the other fellow sees it first.

The doors of opportunity are marked "Push" and "Pull".

Opportunity is frequently overlooked because it disguises itself as work.

The opportunity of a lifetime is seldom so labelled.

A wise man will make more opportunities than he finds. Bacon

The commonest form, one of the most often neglected, and the safest opportunity for the average man to seize, is hard work.

When your automobile engine develops a knock, chances are it's opportunity knocking for some mechanic.

The trouble with opportunity is that it comes disguised as hard work.

## OPTIMIST

"Twixt optimist and pessimist.
The difference is droll;
The optimist ses the donut
The pessimist the hole."

Question: What do they call a woman who runs the motor of her car while waiting for her husband?
Answer: An optimist.

## ORDEAL
What some ideal marriages turn out to be.

## ORGANIZED
Don't confuse this confusion with disorganization . . . because we're not that organized yet.

## ORTHOPEDIST
Orthopedists get all the breaks.

## OVERDRAWN
Husband: I just got a notice from the bank saying I'm overdrawn.

Wife:      Try some other bank . . . they can't all be overdrawn.

## OX
Some cannot manage the calf and still want to carry the ox.

## PAINT
Over bench: "Wet paint. Watch it or wear it."

## PANHANDLER
A fellow walked up to a panhandler and politely remarked: "You're not too old and you look reasonably fit. Why don't you try to get a job?"

"I can't. I inherited this business from my father!"

## PAPERWEIGHTS
A London street-market vendor posts this sign at his stall: "Lovely glass paperweights! The only way to keep housekeeping bills down!"

## PARDON
"I beg your pardon for coming so late."

"My dear, no pardons are needed. You can never come too late."

## PARTING
Two partners had come to the parting of the ways over social and business differences.

"You stole my accounts," shouted one. "You crook."

"And you stole my wife," shouted the other. "You horse thief."

## PASSION

Passion makes idiots of the cleverest men, and makes the biggest idiots clever.

## PATIENCE

Everything comes to him who hustles while he waits.                    Thomas A. Edison

Patience is bitter, but its fruit is sweet.   Rousseau

Beware the fury of a patient man.   John Dryden

It is easy finding reasons why other folks should be patient.

An ounce of patience is worth a pound of brains.

It's important that mothers with small children save something for a rainy day — patience.

Patience is the ability to stand something as long as it happens to the other fellow.

He that hath no patience hath nothing at all.

With patience I the storm sustain,
For sunshine still doth follow rain.

The world is his who has patience.

## PATRIOTISM

Ask not what your country can do for you.
Ask what you can do for your country.
                    John Fitzgerald Kennedy

## PAY

If you pay your servant badly, he will pay himself.

## PAYMENTS

Rod: I've got the worst kind of car trouble anybody could have.

Ron: What kind is it?

Rod: It's when the engine won't start and the payments won't stop.

## PEARLS

A pearl among pebbles is still a pearl.

In deep waters men find great pearls.

## PEEP

He who peeps through the keyhole may lose his eye.

## PEN

There's no wound deeper than a pen can give,
It makes men living dead, and dead men alive.

## PERCEPTION

The heart has eyes which the brain knows nothing of.

## PERFECTION

If a man should happen to reach perfection in this world, he would have to die immediately to enjoy himself.                    Josh Billings

Trifles make perfection, and perfection is no trifle.                    Michelangelo

## PERFUME

Anyone who thinks chemical warfare is something new doesn't know much about women's perfume.

## PERSEVERANCE

Big shots are only little shots who keep shooting.                    Christopher Morley

Consider the postage stamp, my son. It secures success through its ability to stick to one thing till it gets there. Josh Billings

The difference between perseverance and obstinacy is, that one often comes from a strong will, and the other from a strong won't.

Henry Ward Beecher

## PESSIMIST

A pessimist is one who feels badly when he feels good for fear he'll feel worse when he feels better.

No one ought to be so pessimistic he can't see some good in the other fellow's troubles.

A person who grows their own crab grass.

A lot of pessimists go that way from financing optimists.

A pessimist on world conditions had insomnia so bad the sheep were picketing him for shorter hours.

A pessimist complains about the noise made when opportunity knocks.

## PICK

"Believe me, I pick my friends."
"Yes . . . to pieces."

## PICTURE

A picture is a poem without words. Horace

A room hung with pictures is a room hung with thoughts. Joshua Reynolds

## PILOT

The loquacious old gentleman boarded a transport plane and started a conversation with the pilot.

"This plane takes all my courage," he said, "I was almost killed twice in an airplane."

"Once would have been enough," replied the bored pilot.

### PINCH

A man and his little girl were on an overcrowded elevator. Suddenly a lady in front turned around, slapped him and left in a huff. The little girl remarked, "I didn't like her either, Daddy. She stepped on my toe so I pinched her."

### PITCH

He who pitches too high won't get through his song.

### PIZZA

Italian restaurant: "We offer you pizza and quiet."                                    Bennett Cerf

### PLAGIARISM

About the most originality that any writer can hope to achieve honestly is to steal with good judgment.                                      Josh Billings

A certain awkwardness marks the use of borrowed thoughts; but as soon as we have learned what to do with them, they become our own.

Ralph Waldo Emerson

Though old the thought and oft exprest,
'Tis his at last who says it best.

James Russell Lowell

When you take stuff from one writer, it's plagiarism; but when you take it from many writers, it's research.                          Wilson Mizner

### PLANTS

In potted-plant section of Fresno, California, nursery: "Please don't talk to the plants unless you're going to buy."

### PLEASE

Who would please all and please himself too,
Undertakes something he cannot do.

### PLEASURE

What we learn with pleasure we never forget.

### PLUMBER

Walter: Who put that statue under the sink?
Frances: That's no statue . . . that's the plumber.

### POISE

The ability to be ill at ease inconspicuously.

Question: What is the definition of poise?
Answer: The ability to keep talking while the other guy takes the check.

### POLITE

A polite man is one who listens with interest to things he knows all about when they are told to him by a person who knows nothing about them.

### POLITICS

The most promising of all careers.

Politicians are the same all over. They promise to build a bridge even when there is no river.

Nikita Khrushchev

We need a law that will permit a voter to sue a candidate for breach of promise.

All political parties die at last of swallowing their own lies.

The difference between a Republican and a Democrat is: One is IN and the other is OUT.

Some go into politics not to do good, but to do well.

There's one thing the Democrats and Republicans share in common — our money.

Woody Allen

I wish the chemists who successfully removed the lead from gasoline would try the same with our congressmen.

A lobbyist browsing through an encyclopedia the other day came upon a stunning idea. In Ancient Greece, in order to prevent idiot statesmen from passing stupid laws upon the people, at one point in Greek history lawmakers were asked to introduce all new laws while standing on a platform with a rope around their neck. If the law passed, the rope was removed. If it failed, the platform was removed.

Stepped into men's room once and found this sign posted over one of those hot air blowers for drying hands: "Push Button and Listen for a Short Message from the Vice President."

After giving what he considered a stirring, fact-filled campaign speech the candidate looked out at his audience and confidently asked, "Now, are there any questions?"

"Yes," came a voice from the rear. "Who else is running?"

## POLYGON

A heathen who has many wives.

## POOR BOX

The minister's brain is often the "Poor-Box" of the church.

## POSSESSIONS

The wise man carried his possessions within him.

## POSTPONED

When I was a boy, I'd rather be licked twice than postponed once.

## POT-LUCK

If you believe no two women think alike, you've never been to a pot-luck dinner.

## POWER

Power will intoxicate the best hearts, as wine the strongest heads. No man is wise enough, nor good enough to be trusted with unlimited power.

## PRAISE

When we disclaim praise, it is only showing our desire to be praised a second time.

Francois de La Rochefoucauld

He who praises everybody, praises nobody.

Samuel Johnson

I can live for two months on a good compliment.

Mark Twain

Get someone else to blow your horn and the sound will carry twice as far.

Will Rogers

Praise: Letting off esteem.

Try praising your wife, even if it does frighten her at first.

Billy Sunday

It is the greatest possible praise to be praised by a man who is himself deserving of praise.

The best way to get praise is to die.

If our aim is to praise, we should forget to criticize; if our aim is to criticize, we should remember to praise.

Don't praise yourself; let others do it!
>                        Proverbs 27:2

## PRICED

Still as of old men by themselves are priced.
For thirty pieces Judas sold himself, not Christ.

## PRIVILEGED

Under privileged: Not to have remote control for your color television set.

## PRODIGAL

A Sunday School class was being quizzed on the prodigal son. The teacher asked one youngster, "Who was sorry when the prodigal son returned home?"

The boy gave it a lot of deep thought, then said, "The fatted calf."

## PROFESSOR

A textbook wired for sound.

## PROMOTE

One-third of the people in the United States promote, while the other two-thirds provide.
>                        Will Rogers

## PROSPERITY

Something you feel, fold and forward to Washington.

## PROVOCATION

To be able to bear provocation is an argument of great reason, and to forgive it of a great mind.
>                        John Tillotson

## PSYCHIATRIST

I have been coming to your counseling sessions for two years and all you do is listen to what I have to say. You never say anything back.

I didn't have to go to a psychiatrist for that. I could have stayed home with my husband. That's all he does, too.

A man walked into a doctor's office with a pelican on his head.

"You need help immediately," said the doctor.

"I certainly do," said the pelican. "Get this man out from under me."

A big-game hunter recently returned from Africa and went to a psychiatrist. He told the psychiatrist he didn't want to go through analysis, but would pay him $200 for answering two questions.

The psychiatrist said this was highly irregular, but he agreed to do it.

"Is it possible," the hunter asked, "for a man to be in love with an elephant?"

The psychiatrist said, "Absolutely impossible. In all the annals of medicine, I've never heard of it. The whole idea is ridiculous. What's your second question?"

The man then asked meekly,

"Do you know anyone who wants to buy a very large engagement ring?"

Two psychiatrists met in the street. One of them kept brushing his jacket.

"What's new?" asked one.

"Nothing, really, only I have these invisible insects crawling on me!"

"Well," said the other, jumping back, "don't brush them off on me!"

## PUN

A form of humor that causes everyone to groan and is meant to punish the hearers.

## PUNISHMENT

If punishment reaches not the mind it hardens the offender.

This, it seems to me, is the most severe punishment — finding out you are wrong.

Walter Winchell

A wise king stamps out crime by severe punishment. Proverbs 20:26

Punishment that hurts chases evil from the heart. Proverbs 20:30

## PUPPY LOVE

The beginning of a dog's life.

## PURSE

A full purse makes the mouth run over.

## PUSH

Mother: "Did you push your little sister down the stairs?"

Bobby: "I only pushed her down one step. She fell the rest of the way."

## QUARREL

He that blows the coals in quarrels he has nothing to do with has no right to complain if the sparks fly in his face. Benjamin Franklin

I never take my own side in a quarrel.

Robert Frost

Who seeks a quarrel, finds it near at hand.

It takes two to have a quarrel,
But only one to start it.

It is hard to stop a quarrel once it starts, so don't let it begin. Proverbs 17:14

It is an honor for a man to stay out of a fight. Only fools insist on quarreling.

Proverbs 20:3

A quarrelsome man starts fights as easily as a match sets fire to paper. Proverbs 26:21

As the churning of cream yields butter, and a

blow to the nose causes bleeding, so anger causes quarrels.                           Proverbs 30:33

## QUESTION

He must be very ignorant for he answers every question he is asked.

Whoever fears to submit any question to the test of free discussion, loves his own opinion more than the truth.

He who asks a question is a fool for five minutes; he who does not ask a question remains a fool forever.

To a quick question give a slow answer.

## QUOTE

Next to the originator of a good sentence is the first quoter of it.                 Ralph Waldo Emerson

## RADIO

Man has conquered the air but so has our neighbor's radio.

## RAZOR

Jim:  "I got one of those new razors that has twin blades."

Tom:  "How do you like it?"

Jim:  "Shaves good. But now instead of getting nicks, I get ditto marks."

## REAL ESTATE AGENT

The first man to make a mountain out of a molehill was probably a real estate agent.

## REAP

Whatsoever a man soweth, that shall he also reap.                                  Galatians 6:7, KJV

## REBEL

It is senseless to pay tuition to educate a rebel who has no heart for truth.          Proverbs 17:16

It's no fun to be a rebel's father.   Proverbs 17:25

A rebellious son is a grief to his father and a bitter blow to his mother.                    Proverbs 17:25

A son who mistreats his father or mother is a public disgrace.                    Proverbs 19:26

Don't waste your breath on a rebel. He will despise the wisest advice.        Proverbs 23:9

Wisdom is too much for a rebel. He'll not be chosen as a counselor!        Proverbs 24:7

Guide a horse with a whip, a donkey with a bridle, and a rebel with a rod to his back!
                    Proverbs 26:3

When arguing with a rebel, don't use foolish arguments as he does, or you will become as foolish as he is! Prick his conceit with silly replies!
                    Proverbs 26:4-5

To trust a rebel to convey a message is as foolish as cutting off your feet and drinking poison!
                    Proverbs 26:6

Honoring a rebel will backfire like a stone tied to a slingshot!                    Proverbs 26:8

A rebel will misapply an illustration so that its point will no more be felt than a thorn in the hand of a drunkard.                    Proverbs 26:9

The master may get better work from an untrained apprentice than from a skilled rebel.
                    Proverbs 26:10

You can't separate a rebel from his foolishness though you crush him to powder.   Proverbs 27:22

A rebel shouts in anger; a wise man holds his temper in and cools it.          Proverbs 29:11

## RECOUNT

A recount is when the chairman can't believe his ayes.

## RED CROSS

Despite warnings from his guide, an American skiing in Switzerland got separated from his group and fell — uninjured — into a deep crevasse. Several hours later, a rescue party found the yawning pit, and to reassure the stranded skier, shouted down to him, "We're from the Red Cross."

"Sorry," the imperturbable American echoed back, "I already gave at the office!"

## REFORM

The best reformers . . . are those who commence on themselves.

The race could save on half its wasted labor
Would each reform himself and spare his neighbor.

Nothing so needs reforming as other people's habits.          Mark Twain

## REGENERATION

Every generation needs regeneration.

## RELAX

The time to relax is when you don't have time for it.

## RELIEF

My small son approached me the other day and asked if there was anything he could do around the house to earn a little pocket money.

"I can't think of anything."

"Well, then, will you put me on relief?"

## RELIGIOUS FREEDOM

To some people religious freedom means the choice of churches which they may stay away from.

## REMEMBER

A worker was called on the carpet by his supervisor for talking back to his foreman. "Is it true that you called him a liar?"

"Yes, I did."

"Did you call him stupid?"

"Yes."

"Slave driver?"

"Yes."

"And did you call him an opinionated, bullheaded egomaniac?"

"No, but would you write that down so I can remember it?"

## RENT

Bill: How much are they asking for your apartment rent now?

Bob: About twice a day.

## REPENTANCE

Most people repent their sins by thanking God they ain't so wicked as their neighbors.

Josh Billings

True repentance is to cease from sinning.

It is much easier to repent of sins that we have committed than to repent of those that we intend to commit.          Josh Billings

Late repentance is seldom true, but true repentance is never too late.

## REPOSE

Whilst Adam slept, Eve from his side arose:
Strange his first sleep should be his last repose.

## REPROACH

To remind a man of the good turns you have

done him is very much like a reproach.

Demosthenes

The sting of a reproach is the truth of it.

## RESEMBLANCE

"Who is that homely boy who just walked into the room?"

"Why, that's my brother!"

"Oh, you must excuse me. I really hadn't noticed the resemblance."

## RESOLUTION

Good resolutions are simply checks that men draw on a bank where they have no account.

Oscar Wilde

## RESTAURANT

Man in restaurant: "I'll have the $5.00 dinner."

Waitress: "Would you like that on white or dark bread?"

Restaurant chains: Cook-alikes.

## RESURRECTION

Christianity is a religion of the open tomb.

## RETROACTIVE

Wedded Blitz. This letter-to-the-editor appeared in a local newspaper: "I have read recently that the word 'obey' is now being omitted from the wedding ceremony. May I ask if you think the new wording for the wedding service is retroactive?"

## REVENUE

Internal Revenue man, eyeing taxpayer's expense claims: "Shall we go over this item by item or would you prefer to chicken out right now?"

## REVERSE REASON

She married him because he was such a "dominating man," she divorced him because he was such a "Dominating male."

He married her because she was so "fragile and petite," he divorced her becaue she was so "weak and helpless."

She married him because "he knows how to provide a good living," she divorced him because "all he thinks about is business."

He married her because "she reminds me of my mother," he divorced her because "she's getting more like her mother every day."

She married him because he was "happy and romantic," she divorced him because he was "shiftless and fun-loving."

He married her because she was "steady and sensible," he divorced her because she was "boring and dull."

She married him because he was "the life of the party," she divorced him because "he never wants to come home from a party."

## REVOLUTION

Every revolution was first a thought in one man's mind.

## RICH

Beverly: A scientist says that what we eat we become.

Melba: Oh, boy. Let's order something rich.

Trying to get rich quick is evil and leads to poverty.
Proverbs 28:22

Better to live rich than to die rich.

## RICH RELATIVES

The kin we love to touch.

Question: What type of person lives the longest?

Answer: A rich relative.

## RIDICULE
Ridicule is the first and last argument of fools.

## RIGHTS
A man is endowed with certain inalienable rights all of which he must fight for.

The good man knows the poor man's rights; the godless don't care.                    Proverbs 29:7

Every right implies a responsibility; every opportunity, an obligation; every possession, a duty.

## ROBBED
The teller had just been robbed for the third time by the same man, and the police officer was asking if he had noticed anything specific about the criminal.

"Yes," said the teller, "he seems to be better dressed each time."

## ROD
Fuller said: "He that will not use the rod on his child, his child shall be used as a rod on him."

## ROOKIE
First Rookie:      "I feel like punching that sarge in the nose again!"

Second Rookie:   "What do you mean, again?"

First Rookie:      "Well, I felt like it yesterday, too."

## RUDDER
He who will not answer to the rudder, must answer to the rocks.

The first hour of the morning is the rudder of the day.                    H.W. Beecher

## RUMOR
A rumor goes in one ear and out many mouths.

Rumor is one thing that gets thicker as you spread it.

There is no such thing as an idle rumor.

What dainty morsels rumors are. They are eaten with great relish!               Proverbs 18:8

## RUSH HOUR
When the traffic stands still.

## SABLE
The skin girls love to touch.

## SAIL
Don't carry too much sail.

## SALT
A small boy was watching his mother change the baby. When she overlooked sprinkling the tot's backside with talcum powder and hurried him into his diaper, the five-year-old reproved her sharply, "Hey, Mom, you forgot to salt him."

## SANTA CLAUS
The three stages of man: he believes in Santa Claus; he does not believe in Santa Claus; he is Santa Claus.

## SARCASM
Sarcasm is jealousy in bold disguise.

Sarcasm — getting an edge in wordwise.

Sarcasm: quip lash.

## SATISFACTION
Telling the truth gives a man great satisfaction, and hard work returns many blessings to him.
                                               Proverbs 12:14

## SAVER
A saver grows rich by seeming poor, a spender grows poor by seeming rich.

## SCAFFOLDING
Ken: My uncle fell off a scaffolding and

was killed.

Bob: What was he doing up on the scaffolding?

Ken: Getting hanged.

## SCHOOL DAYS

School days are the best days of your life . . . provided your children are old enough to go.

## SCRATCHING

A teacher called on the mother of a boy who came to school in a dirty condition.

"Can you explain," she asked, "how he gets his nails so dirty?"

"I expect that's because he's always scratching himself," replied the fond mother.

## SEASICK

Question: What's green, has two legs, and a trunk?

Answer: A seasick traveler.

## SECRET

People keep a secret well but sometimes it takes quite a few of them to do it.

If you wish another to keep your secret, just keep it yourself.                    Seneca

What we give to others to keep for us.

A secret known to be concealed,
Like money suspected in a field,
Is half discovered.

Some people's idea of keeping a secret is to refuse to tell who told it to them.

Some people always think it takes two to keep a secret.

Three may keep a secret, if two of them are dead.                    Franklin

If you really want to keep a secret, you don't need any help.

A secret is a weapon and a friend.

## SECRETIVE

Teacher: In your homework last night, what did you find out about the salivary glands?

Student: I couldn't find out a thing. They're so secretive.

## SELF-CONTROL

Keep yourself from the opportunity God will keep you from the sins it leads to.

Greater is he who conquers himself than he who conquers a thousand.

It is better to be slow-tempered than famous; it is better to have self-control than to control an army.

Proverbs 16:32

A man without self-control is as defenseless as a city with broken-down walls.

Proverbs 16:32

## SELFISH

SEL-FISH is the most dangerous fish existing.

## SELF-KNOWLEDGE

When you decide to know yourself, you may find the acquaintance isn't worth the effort.

To know yourself well, is to esteem yourself little.

## SENATORS

Rome had senators, that's why it declined.

## SENSIBLE

A sensible son gladdens his father. A rebellious son saddens his mother.

Proverbs 15:20

Bill:     You look like a nice, sensible, well-adjusted girl. Let's go steady.

Sharon:  No. I'm just as nice, sensible, and well-adjusted as I look.

## SEPARATES

The thing that separates the men from the boys is the price of auto insurance.

## SERMON

A sermon's length is not its strength.

One beautiful Sunday morning, a minister announced to his congregation: "My good people, I have here in my hands three sermons — a $100 sermon that lasts five minutes, a $50 sermon that lasts 15 minutes and a $10 sermon that lasts a full hour. Now, we'll take the collection and see which one I'll deliver."

The average man's idea of a good sermon is one that goes over his head — and hits one of his neighbors.

## SERVICE

A man who had been married for ten years was consulting a marriage counselor, "When I was first married, I was very happy. I'd come home from a hard day down at the shop, and my little dog would race around barking, and my wife would brings my slippers. Now everything's changed. When I come home, my dog brings my slippers, and my wife barks at me."

"I don't know what you're complaining about," said the counselor. "You're still getting the same service."

He who serves well need not fear to ask his wages.

## SEWAGE

The Red Sea and the Mediterranean are connected by the Sewage Canal.

## SHARE

Why is it a woman is willing to share her whole life with her husband — but not her closet space?

## SHIP

A ship in harbor is safe, but that is not what ships are built for.

"It's no use waiting for your ship to come in unless you have one out."

## SHOCK

Cross an electric eel with a sponge and you'll have shock absorbers.

## SHOE REPAIR

While rummaging through his attic, a man found a shoe repair ticket that was nine years old. Figuring that he had nothing to lose, he went to the shop and presented the ticket to the proprietor, who reluctantly began a search for the unclaimed shoes. After ten minutes, the owner reappeared and handed back the ticket.

"Well," asked the customer, "did you find the pair?"

"Yes," replied the shop owner. "They'll be ready Tuesday."

## SHOPPING

Grocery shopping: Staple chase.

## SHORT CUT

A short cut is often the longest way.

## SHIRT-SLEEVE

People who wear short-sleeve shirts can't make off-the-cuff remarks.

## SHOT

"I shot my dog."

"Was he mad?"
"Well, it didn't seem to exactly please him."

## SIDE

Sir, my concern is not whether God is on our side; my great concern is to be on God's side, for God is always right.                                    Lincoln

## SIGN

A dollar sign has been described as a capital S which has been double-crossed.

"What sign were you born under?"
"Quiet — Hospital Zone."

Outside a house in Sussex, England: "Beware of owner. Never mind the dog."

Sign outside of house rented by gypsies:
FORTUNES TOLD: $2.00: PSYCHOANALYSIS 75 CENTS EXTRA.

Sign in store window:
FRESH EGGS PACKED IN NO-DEPOSIT, NO-RETURN, BIODEGRADABLE SHELLS.

Sign outside house in the city:
TRESPASSERS WILL BE PROSECUTED TO THE FULL EXTENT OF ONE GERMAN SHEPHERD.

Sign on garbage truck:
SATISFACTION GUARANTEED, OR DOUBLE YOUR GARBAGE BACK.

## SILENCE

Sometimes silence is not golden — just yellow.

If you keep your mouth shut you will never put your foot in it.

Silence is foolish if we are wise, but wise if we are foolish.

Silence is one of the hardest arguments to refute.
Josh Billings

Talking comes by nature, silence by wisdom.

Most people are quite happy to suffer in silence, if they are sure everybody knows they are doing it.

You hesitate to stab me with a word,
And know not silence is the sharper sword.

Silence is the only substitute for brains.

As we must account for every idle word, so must we for every idle silence.

No one is so hard to answer as a fellow who keeps his mouth shut.

Silence is sometimes the severest criticism.

The only substitute for wisdom is silence.

## SIN

He who is without sin among you, let him be the first to throw a stone at her.
John 8:7, NAS

Confess your sins to the Lord, and you will be forgiven; confess them to men, and you will be laughed at.
Josh Billings

## SINKING FUND

We had a sinking fund. It just went down for the third time.

## SKILLFUL

Learn of the skillful: he that teaches himself hath a fool for a master.

## SLEEPING PILLS

The new bride stopped at the druggist's for a refill of an order of sleeping pills. "I don't know what I'd do without them. I'd never get any rest."

"Be sure not to take too many," cautioned the druggist.

"Me?" said the bride in surprise. "Oh, I never take them. I give them to my husband."

## SLOW

"Look here, private, this man beside you on this fatigue detail is doing twice the work you are."

"I know, sarge. That's what I've been telling him for the last hour, but he won't slow down."

## SPHINX

Professor: "Jones, can you tell me who built the Sphinx?"

Student: "I-I-I did know, sir, but I've forgotten!"

Professor: "Great guns, what a calamity! The only man living who knows, and he has forgotten!"

## SPLINTERS

Chet: How did you get your hand full of splinters?

Jack: I was out hunting . . . and caught a timber wolf bare-handed.

## SPOKESMAN

He who talks like a big wheel may be only a spokesman.

## SPORT CARS

One nice thing about small sport cars . . . if you flood the carburetor, you can just put the car over your shoulder and burp it.

## SPRINGTIME

On the first day of springtime my true love gave to me: five packs of seed, four sacks of fertilizer, three cans of weed killer, two bottles of insect spray, and a pruning knife for the pear tree.

## STARS

The stars make no noise.

## STARTING

The journey of a thousand miles begins with one pace.

## STATION

A janitor who worked in a railroad station decided to get married in a huge room on the upper floor of the station. So many friends and kinfolk showed up, their combined weight caused the building to collapse. Moral of the story: Never marry above your station.

## STEADY

Bill: "I'm a steady worker."
Bob: "Yeah, and if you were any steadier, you would be motionless."

## STEAM

Too many people work up a head of steam before they find out what's cooking.

## STONE

"My husband didn't leave a bit of insurance."

"Then where did you get that gorgeous diamond ring?"

"Well, he left $1,000 for his casket and $5,000 for a stone. This is the stone."

## STORY

We like the fellow who says he is going to make a long story short, and does.

## STRANGERS

Be not forgetful to entertain strangers: for thereby some have entertained angels unawares.

Hebrews 13:2, KJV

## STRIFE

If you want to avoid domestic strife, don't marry in January ... and that goes for the other months, too.

A dry crust eaten in peace is better than steak everyday along with argument and strife.

Proverbs 17:1

## STUDY

The more we study the more we discover our ignorance.

## STUPID

Are you naturally stupid or did a Cuban hijack your brain?

## SUFFER

Great souls suffer in silence.

Some persons won't suffer in silence because that would take the pleasure out of it.

## SUGAR

Ben: "One of our little pigs was sick so I gave him some sugar."

Dan: "Sugar! What for?"

Ben: "Haven't you ever heard of sugar-cured ham?"

## SUICIDE

The last thing a person should do.

## SULTAN

Sultan to small boy: "Go ask one of your mothers."

## SUNDAY SCHOOL

The road to success is dotted with many tempting parking places.

Son: Dad, did you go to Sunday School when you were young?

Dad: Never missed a Sunday.

Son: Bet it won't do me any good either.

## SUPERIORITY

My kid sister has a superiority complex . . . she thinks she's almost as good as me.

## SURLY

Cheerful people, the doctors say, resist disease better than the glum ones. In other words, the surly bird catches the germ.

## SURRENDER

Another word for engagement.

## SWAP

Seems that a tribal chieftain's daughter was offered as a bride to the son of a neighboring potentate in exchange for two cows and four sheep. The big swap was to be effected on the shore of the stream that separated the two tribes. Pop and his daughter showed up at the appointed time only to discover that the groom and his livestock were on the other side of the stream. The father grunted, "The fool doesn't know which side his bride is bartered on."

## SWEEP

A new broom sweeps well, but an old one is best for the corners.

## SWELL-HEAD

Nature's frantic effort to fill a vacuum.

## TALEBEARER

A talehearer is brother to a talebearer.

## TALKER

A great talker may be no fool, but he is one that relies on him.

Two great talkers will not travel far together.

## TALKING

Long talking begets short hearing.

The other day I was driving under the influence

of my husband. He talks and talks. He gets two thousand words to the gallon.

Son: What do you call it when one is talking?
Dad: Monologue.
Son: What do you call it when two women are talking?
Dad: Cat-alogue.

Young Tom told his father that when he grew up, he wanted to drive a big army tank.

"Well, Son," said his dad, "if that's what you want to do, I certainly won't stand in your way."

## TASKS

Some tasks have to be put off dozens of times before they will completely slip your mind.

## TAX

The income tax has made more liars out of the American people than gold has.          Will Rogers

What is the difference between a taxidermist and a tax collector?

The taxidermist takes only your skin. Mark Twain

The tax collector must love poor people — he's creating so many of them.

Nothing makes time pass more quickly than an income tax installment every three months.

## TAX COLLECTOR

The difference between a tax collector and a taxidermist is that the taxidermist leaves the hide intact.

## TAXES

The reward for saving your money is being able to pay your taxes without borrowing.

An American can consider himself a success

when it costs him more to support the government than to support a wife and children.

It's awfully difficult to believe that only about 200 years ago we went to war to avoid taxation.

I'm gonna put all my money into taxes. They're sure to go up.

Income Tax Song: "Everything I have is yours."

April 15 should be called Taxgiving day.

Taxpayer: I always pay my income taxes all at once.
Tax
Collector: But you are allowed to pay it in quarterly installments.
Taxpayer: I know it, but my heart can't stand it four times a year.

## TEA

Three Englishmen stopped at a restaurant for a spot of tea. The waiter appeared with pad and pencil.

"I'll have a glass of weak tea," ordered the first.

"I'll have tea, too," said the second, "but very strong with two pieces of lemon."

"Tea for me, too, please," said the third. But be sure the glass is absolutely clean."

In a short time the waiter was back with the order. "All right," he asked. "Which one gets the clean glass?"

## TEARS

The most efficient water power in the world — women's tears.

## TEENAGERS

"What did your teenage daughter do all summer?"

"Her hair and her nails!"

Oh, to be only half as wonderful as my child thought I was. And only half as stupid as my teenager thinks I am.

Father to teenage daughter: "I want you home by 11 o'clock."
"But Daddy, I'm no longer a child."
"I know, that's why I want you home by 11."

A teenager is someone who can eat his heart out without affecting his appetite.

Dialogue between teenager and parent:
"I'm off to the party."
"Well, have a good time."
"Look, Pop, don't tell me what to do."

If you live in a house full of teenagers, it is not necessary to ask for whom the bell tolls. It's not for you.

Dad: Did you use the car last night?
Son: Yes, Dad. I took some of the boys for a ride.
Dad: Well, tell them I found two of their lipsticks.

About the time the bedtime stories are televised, many youngsters are going out for the evening.

## TELEPHONE

Mother:    Is this telephone call really necessary?
Daughter: How can I tell till I've made it?

Did you hear about the teenager who plans to run away from home just as soon as she gets a long enough telephone extension cord?

## TEMPER

There is more hope for a fool than for a man of quick temper.                    Proverbs 29:20

Something you never lose, because it is always there when you need it.

The worst-tempered people I've ever met were people who knew they were wrong.

A tart temper never mellows with age; and a sharp tongue is the only edged tool that grows keener with constant use.          Washingtin Irving

Men lose their tempers in defending their taste.
Ralph Waldo Emerson

Keep your temper; no one else wants it.

A wise man controls his temper. He knows that anger causes mistakes.          Proverbs 14:29

A quick-tempered man starts fights; a cool-tempered man tries to stop them.
Proverbs 15:18

## TENDER
Question:  Why did the locomotive refuse to sit?
Answer:    Because it had a tender behind.

## TEST
The test: Could I? Would I? Should I? and Will I?

## THEOLOGY
Division has done more to hide Christ from the view of all men than all the infidelity that has ever been spoken.

## THINK
The less a man thinks, the more he talks.

The reason some of us find it difficult to think is that we haven't had any previous experience.

There are two kinds of thinkers in the world. Those who think they can and those who think they can't . . . and they're both right.

The person who thinks before he speaks is silent most of the time.

## THOUGHT

You are today what you thought yesterday.

The main reason that some of us get lost in thought is that it is such unfamiliar territory.

## THREATEN

Who threatens most is he who most doth fear.

## TIGER

He who rides a tiger is afraid to dismount.

## TIGHT

He's so tight he keeps five dollar bills folded so long that Lincoln gets ingrown whiskers.

## TITLE

In an age when everyone seems to be playing the name game of glorifying job titles, the man in charge of the meat department at a store in Wichita Falls, Texas, deserves a round of applause. On his weekly time card he describes his position as "Meat Head."

## TOE

Nothing is harder to do secretly than stub your toe.

## TOM

"My name is T-t-t-t-tom."
"I'll call you Tom for short."

## TONGUE

The tongue is the ambassador of the heart.

Hold your tongue, and hold your friend.

The tongue is in a wet place, and easily slips.

A sharp tongue is the only edge tool that grows keener with constant use.        Washington Irving

Many have fallen by the edge of the sword; but not so many as have fallen by the tongue.

Don't let your tongue say what your head may pay for.

## TOOTHACHE

There was never yet philosopher
That could endure the toothache patiently.
Shakespeare

## TOTAL

The sum total of our national debt is some total.

## TOURIST

A person who travels 1,000 miles to get a picture of himself standing by his car.

## TRAIN OF THOUGHT

"Be quiet. You're interrupting my train of thought."
"Let me know when it comes to a station."

## TRAP

The man who sets a trap for others will get caught in it himself. Roll a boulder down on someone, and it will roll back and crush you.
Proverbs 26:27

## TRIALS

A gem cannot be polished without friction, nor a man perfected without trials.

## TRIUMPH

Triumph is just "umph" added to "try."

## TRUST

Trust in your money and down you go! Trust in God and flourish as a tree!        Proverbs 11:28

In God we trust — all others pay cash.

Don't pick me up before I fall down.

## TRUSTWORTHY

A servant is known by his master's absence.

## TRUTHFULNESS

There's no limit to the height a man can attain by remaining on the level.

## TRYING

Mother: "Johnny, this isn't a very good report card. Are you trying?"

Johnny: "Yes, my teacher said I am the most trying boy in the class."

Mother, having finally tucked a small boy into bed after an unusually trying day: "Well, I've worked today from son-up to son-down!"

## TWINS

Melba: I guess your husband was pleased when he found himself the father of twin boys.

Pam: Was he! He went around grinning from heir to heir.

Insult added to injury.

## UNAWARE

Question: What is the meaning of the word "unaware"?

Answer: Unaware is what you put on first and take off last.

## UNBALANCED

They say that one in every four Americans is unbalanced. Think of your three closest friends. If they seem OK, then you're in trouble.

## UNDERWEAR

Something that creeps up on you.

## UNION

Man filling out an application for union membership:"Does this union have any death benefits?"

"Sure does," replied the union representative. "When you die you don't have to pay any more dues."

## UNIVERSITY

Universities are full of knowledge; the freshmen bring a little in and the seniors take none away, and knowledge accumulates.

## UNKEMPT

A guy goes to the doctor and the doctor says, "You have the dirtiest, most unkempt, uncivilized body I have ever seen." The patient says, "That's funny, that's what the other doctor told me yesterday." "Then why did you come to see me?" The patient answers, "I wanted a second opinion."

## UNRELIABLE

An unreliable messenger can cause a lot of trouble. Reliable communication permits progress.

Proverbs 13:17

Putting confidence in an unreliable man is like chewing with a sore tooth, or trying to run on a broken foot.                    Proverbs 25:19

## VACATION

A period of travel and relaxation when you take twice the clothes and half the money you need.

No man needs a vacation so much as the man who has just had one.

A vacation resort is where you go when you are worn out and where you come back from a complete wreck.

The bigger the summer vacation the harder the fall.

## VALUE

If a man empties his purse into his head, no one can take it from him.                    Franklin

## VASE

Benjie: "Mom, do you remember that vase you
            always worried I would break?"
Mom: "Yes, what about it?"
Benjie: "Your worries are over."

## VENGEANCE

Deep vengeance is the daughter of deep silence.

Avenge not yourselves, but rather give place unto wrath: for it is written, Vengeance is mine; I will repay, saith the Lord.

                         Romans 12:19, KJV

## VERBOSITY

Inebriated with the exuberance of his own ver-bosity.                    Benjamin Disraeli

## VICTORY

Go ahead and prepare for the conflict, but vic-tory comes from God.              Proverbs 21:31

## VIOLENCE

Nothing good ever comes of violence.
                         Martin Luther

## VISION

One may have good eyes, and see nothing.

Don't call the world dirty because you have forgotten to clean your glasses.

## VOICE

Pretty Young Student: "Professor Boschovich, do you think I will ever be able to do anything with my voice?"

Weary Teacher: "Well it might come in handy in case of fire or shipwreck."

## VOMIT

As a dog returns to his vomit, so a fool repeats his folly.                    Proverbs 26:11

## WAITER

Diner: Is it customary to tip the waiter in this restaurant?

Waiter: Why . . . ah . . . yes, sir.

Diner: Then hand me a tip. I've waited almost an hour for that steak I ordered.

A waiter is one that believes that money grows on trays.

## WAR

Another thing against war is that it seldom if ever kills off the right people.

## WASHINGTON

Washington, D.C.: Fund city.

## WATERMELONS

Fruit and vegetable market: "Best watermelons you ever seed."

Two watermelons cannot be held under one arm.

## WEAKNESS

Don't judge your wife too harshly for her weaknesses. If she didn't have them, chances are she would never have married you.

## WEATHER

Don't knock the weather; nine-tenths of the people couldn't start a conversation if it didn't change once in a while.

Everybody talks about the weather but nobody does anything about it.

Probably the last completely accurate weather forecast was when God told Noah there was a 100 percent chance of precipitation.

## WEDLOCK

The chain of wedlock is so heavy that it takes two to carry it — sometimes three.

Dumas

## WEEVILS

Two boll weevils came from the country to the city. One became rich and famous. The other remained the lesser of the two weevils.

## WEIGHT

Some women would be more spic if they had less span.

## WHISTLED

The biggest adjustment a bride must make is getting used to being whistled for instead of at.

## WHITE HOUSE

Honorable mansion.

## WICKEDNESS

God bears with the wicked, but not forever.

Miguel de Cervantes

If men are so wicked with religion, what would they be without it?        Franklin

Wickedness loves company — and leads others into sin.        Proverbs 16:29

## WIVES

Men do not know their wives well; but wives know their husbands perfectly.

## WILL

Lawyer, reading a wise old man's will to the relatives. "And being of sound mind, I spent every dollar I had."

A rich uncle died and a line in his will read as follows: "I leave to my beloved nephew all the money he owes me."

## WIND

No wind is a good wind if you don't know where the harbor is.

A tourist traveling through western Kansas saw a man sitting by the ruins of a house that had been blown away.

"Was this your house, my friend?" he asked sympathetically.

"Yep."

"Any of your family blown away with the house?"

"Yes, wife and four kids."

"Great Scot, man, why aren't you hunting for them?"

"Well, stranger, I've been in this country quite a spell. The wind's due to change this afternoon. So I figure I might as well wait here till it brings 'em back."

## WINE-AGE

People are like wine — age sours the bad and improves the good.

## WISDOM

The older I grow the more I distrust the familiar doctrine that age brings wisdom.

A wise youth accepts his father's rebuke; a young mocker doesn't.    Proverbs 13:1

A wise man doesn't display his knowledge, but a fool displays his foolishness.

Proverbs 12:23

How much better is wisdom than gold, and understanding than silver!    Proverbs 16:16

The wise man saves for the future, but the foolish man spends whatever he gets.

Proverbs 21:20

He that gets money before he gets wit,
Will be but a short while master of it.

A wise man is mightier than a strong man.
Wisdom is mightier than strength.

Proverbs 24:5

The fear of the Lord is the beginning of wisdom.

Psalms 111:10,KJV

In much wisdom is much grief.

Ecclesiastes 1:18,KJV

The price of wisdom is above rubies.

Job 28:18,KJV

A single conversation across the table with a
wise man is worth a month's study of books.

It is wit to pick a lock, and steal a horse, but
wisdom to let it alone.

My son, honey whets the appetite, and so does
wisdom! When you enjoy becoming wise, there is
hope for you! A bright future lies ahead!

Proverbs 24:13-14

## WISE MAN

A wise man thinks ahead; a fool doesn't and
even brags about it!          Proverbs 13:16

The advice of a wise man refreshes like water
from a mountain spring. Those accepting it
become aware of the pitfalls on ahead.

Proverbs 13:14

A wise man is cautious and avoids danger; a
fool plunges ahead with great confidence.

Proverbs 14:16

A wise man restrains his anger and overlooks insults. This is to his credit.        Proverbs 19:11

## WIT

A fellow who thinks he's a wit is usually half right.

Wit is the salt of the conversation, not the food.

The next best thing to being witty one's self, is to be able to quote another's wit.

He who has provoked the shaft of wit, cannot complain that he smarts from it.

Samuel Johnson

To be witty is not enough. One must possess sufficient wit to avoid having too much of it.

Wit is not always grinning.

Wit without wisdom is salt without meat.

All wit is not wisdom.

Wit without discretion is a sword in the hand of a fool.

Use your wit as a buckler, not as a sword.

Wit is a good servant but a bad master.

Talleyrand

The wittiest man laughs least.

A fool attempting to be witty
Is an object of profoundest pity.

## WOLF

A girl can be scared to death by a mouse or a

spider, but she's often too willing to take her chances with a wolf.

## WOMEN

A fallen woman is a mother whose children didn't pick up their toys.

You see, dear, it is not true that woman was made from man's rib; she was really made from his funny bone.

The way to fight a woman is with your hat. Grab it and run.                    John Barrymore

Being a woman is a terribly difficult task since it consists principally in dealing with men.

On one issue, at least, men and women agree; they both distrust women.

Woman begins by resisting man's advances and ends by blocking his retreat.

A good woman inspires a man, a brilliant woman interests him, a beautiful woman fascinates him — but a sympathetic woman gets him.

A woman without religion is as a flower without scent.

A wise woman builds her house, while a foolish woman tears hers down by her own efforts.
                                          Proverbs 14:1

## WOMEN'S LIB

Adam-smasher.

At a holiday party, the Brooklyn Women's Bar Association staged a revue called "God Created Adam — Then Corrected Her Mistake."

## WOOL

There was the man who owned a lot of sheep and wanted to take them over a river that was all ice, but the woman who owned the river said, "No." So he promised to marry her and that's how he pulled the wool over her ice.

## WORK

Hard work brings prosperity; playing around brings poverty.                    Proverbs 28:19

Don't bother to boast of our work to others; the work itself has a much better voice.

No bees, no honey;
No work; no money.

The lazy man won't go out and work. "There might be a lion outside," he says.
                                    Proverbs 26:13

Work brings profit; talk brings poverty!
                                    Proverbs 14:23

Pursue thy work without delay,
For the short hours run fast away.

Steady plodding brings prosperity; hasty speculation brings poverty.
                                    Proverbs 21:5

Modern day teenager to Millionaire: "What's the first secret of your success?"
"Hard work."
"What's the second one?"

God gives every bird its food, but does not throw it into the nest.

Half the people like to work and the other half don't, or maybe it's the other way 'round.

Jim: It's no disgrace to work.
Tim: That's what I tell my wife.

Lady: Why don't you work? Hard work never
    killed anyone.
Bum: You're wrong, lady. I lost both of my
    wives that way.

Work is the yeast that raises the dough.

It's probably true that hard work is a tonic, but many people never get sick enough to try the remedy.

## WORLD'S CHAMPIONSHIP

"I remember my wedding day very distinctly," said the elderly gentleman. "I carried my new bride across the threshold of our little house and said, 'Honey, this is your and my little world.'"

"And I suppose you've lived happily ever after?" "We've been fighting for the world's championship ever since."

## WORRY

Worry is interest paid on trouble before it is due.

Don't tell me that worry doesn't do any good. I know better. The things I worry about don't happen.

Worry gives a small thing a big shadow.

The reason why worry kills more people than work is that more people worry than work.

                                    Robert Frost

I am an old man and have known a great many troubles, but most of them never happened.

                                    Mark Twain

To worry about tomorrow is to be unhappy today.

To carry care to bed is to sleep with a pack on your back.

There are two days about which nobody should ever worry, and these are yesterday and tomorrow.

Worry grows lushly in the soil of its sorrow; it only saps today of its joy.

We probably wouldn't worry about what people think of us if we could know how seldom they do.

The greatest fool is he who worries about what he cannot help.

## WORTH

It's not what you pay a man, but what he costs you that counts.                        Will Rogers

## WRECKED

Pretty young girl to friend: "Not only has Jack broken my heart and wrecked my whole life, but he has spoiled my entire evening!"

## WRINKLES

If you would keep the wrinkles out of your face, keep sunshine in your heart.

## WRONG

The man who says "I may be wrong, but . . ." does not believe there can be any such possibility.

## YES

A married woman's last word.

# GLOSSARY

## Other Books by Bob Phillips

- ◆ *World's Greatest Collection of Clean Jokes*
- ◆ *More Good Clean Jokes*
- ◆ *The Last of the Good Clean Jokes*
- ◆ *The Return of the Good Clean Jokes*
- ◆ *The All American Joke Book*
- ◆ *The World's Greatest Collection of Heavenly Humor*
- ◆ *The World's Greatest Collection of Riddles and Daffy Definitions*
- ◆ *The World's Greatest Collection of Knock, Knock Jokes and Tongue Twisters*
- ◆ *The Best of the Good Clean Jokes*
- ◆ *Wit and Wisdom*
- ◆ *Humor Is Tremendous*
- ◆ *The All New Clean Joke Book*
- ◆ *Good Clean Jokes for Kids*
- ◆ *The Encyclopedia of Good Clean Jokes*
- ◆ *Bible Fun*
- ◆ *Heavenly Fun*
- ◆ *The Ultimate Bible Trivia Challenge*
- ◆ *The Little Book of Bible Trivia*
- ◆ *How Can I Be Sure? A Pre-Marriage Inventory*
- ◆ *Anger Is a Choice*
- ◆ *Redi-Reference*
- ◆ *Redi-Reference Daily Bible Reading Plan*
- ◆ *The Delicate Art of Dancing with Porcupines*
- ◆ *Powerful Thinking for Powerful Living*
- ◆ *God's Hand Over Hume*
- ◆ *Praise Is a Three-Lettered Word—Joy*
- ◆ *The Handbook for Headache Relief*